133 BAR COOKIE RECIPES FROM THE HIGH COUNTRY

Here, from the High Country, is a collection of great tasting, quick and easy bar cookie recipes. No need for fancy rolling, cutting, or spooning out on cookie sheets. Just spread them in the pan, pop them in the oven and they're ready to be eaten in just a few minutes.

These recipes have been specially formulated for Hungarian® High Altitude® flour, the long time favorite for High Country baking. It takes a special wheat to make a special flour like Hungarian® High Altitude®... the hard spring wheat grown in Colorado, the Dakotas, and Montana. Hungarian flour is specially milled for the kind of baking made famous in the High Country.

Make your kitchen famous for that never-empty cookie jar, filled with a variety of bar cookies. It's easy with Hungarian® High Altitude® flour. Living in the high country—there's nothing like it.

KNOW YOUR INGRE-DIENTS

"Using good and the correct ingredients is an important step for the best baked products."

FLOUR: All the recipes have been developed for use with HUNGARIAN®HIGH ALTITUDE®FLOUR. Only when this flour is used can we guarantee success. To measure accurately, spoon it lightly from sack or canister into measuring cup (the nested type), then level off across the top with metal spatula.

BROWN SUGAR: If brown sugar is lumpy, roll between sheets of waxed paper or smash lumps with fingers. Lumps will melt during baking and leave holes in baked product. When measuring, pack brown sugar into cup. It should keep shape of the cup when turned out.

POWDERED (CONFECTIONERS') SUGAR: Spoon sugar lightly into measuring cup and level off with metal spatula.

BUTTER AND MARGARINE: Regular (including soft) margarine and butter may be used interchangeably in most recipes. Whipped margarines and margarine substitutes are not generally recommended for use in baking, unless the recipes have been specifically developed for them. Margarine will not brown so do not use in recipes calling for browned butter. Unless otherwise directed it is easier to cream, cut or blend butter with other ingredients if it is at room temperature. Most margarines are soft enough to mix or blend at refrigerator temperature.

SHORTENING in recipes refers to a homogenized vegetable-type shortening. Store these shortenings at room temperature so they are soft, pliable and cream easily.

BAKING POWDER loses its leavening action and should never be kept more than a year after the can is opened. Date the can when opened.

UNSWEETENED CHOCOLATE: Use either the packets of pre-melted chocolate or the solid chocolate. One square or ounce is equal to 1 envelope of the pre-melted chocolate.

CHOCOLATE CHIPS: Two types of chips are available — the pure chocolate and the chocolate flavored. The latter is more economical to use. The chocolate flavored product is made from cocoa, vegetable shortening and sugar. It does not contain an artificial chocolate. The chocolate flavored have a milder chocolate flavor than the semi-sweet chips made from chocolate and cocoa butter. When melted the chocolate flavored chips are sometimes stiffer. If too thick to spread or mix in, add a tablespoon or two of vegetable shortening. When melting any kind of chocolate chips with a small amount of shortening, always use a vegetable shortening. The water in the butter will cause the melted chips to solidify.

NOTE: Do not change ingredient amounts basic to the recipes. Nuts in many recipes can be omitted. If chocolate chips and coconut are not a basic part of the recipe, smaller quantities can be used.

NEW FAVORITES

If you're looking for a new twist to an old favorite or a completely new idea to add to your recipe collection, you'll find them here. All made easy to make. In this section and throughout the book you'll find new recipes for the bake sale or recipe exchange.

TOASTY COCONUT BARS

"Maple flavored butter bars that are toasty with coconut."

BAKE: 360° F. for 25 to 30 minutes

MAKES: 13x9-inch pan

¾ cup butter or margarine	1⅔ cups Hungarian®High
½ cup packed brown sugar	Altitude® Flour
¼ cup powdered sugar	1 cup flaked coconut
½ teaspoon maple flavoring	

Cream together butter, sugars and maple flavoring. Blend in flour. Press into bottom of ungreased 13x9-inch pan. Sprinkle with coconut; press down firmly with fork.

Bake at 360° F. for 25 to 30 minutes, or until coconut is golden brown. Cut into squares while warm.

TOASTY CHIP BARS

Add ½ cup **chocolate chips** with flour.

NUTTY BARS

Substitute ¾ cup **almond slices** or chopped pecans for the coconut.

CHOCOLATE FROSTIES

Sprinkle hot bars with 1 cup (6 oz.) **milk chocolate** or **semi-sweet chocolate chips.** When soft, spread to frost.

PEANUT BUTTER CANDY BARS

"Tastes just like a favorite candy bar — crunchy on the bottom and on top, a layer of chocolate and peanut butter."

BAKE: 375° F. for 20 to 25 minutes

MAKES: 13x9-inch pan

¾ cup butter or margarine	1 teaspoon vanilla
2 cups quick-cooking rolled oats	½ teaspoon soda
1¼ cups Hungarian® High Altitude® Flour	⅓ cup dark corn syrup
1 cup packed brown sugar	½ cup peanut butter
1 teaspoon salt	½ to 1 cup chocolate chips

Melt butter in saucepan. Add remaining ingredients except peanut butter and chocolate chips. Press into bottom of greased 13x9-inch pan.

Bake at 375° F. for 20 to 25 minutes, or until light golden brown. (Do not overbake.) Spoon peanut butter over hot bars and sprinkle with chocolate chips. When soft, spread to frost.

Tip: If you want a layer of peanut butter and a chocolate glaze on top, do this. Spread peanut butter over hot bars. Melt chocolate chips with 2 tablespoons shortening over hot water. Drizzle over peanut butter.

PEANUT BUTTER SQUARES

"Great cookies for the kids' after school snack — double peanut butter treat."

BAKE: 350° F. for 20 to 25 minutes

MAKES: 13x9-inch pan

½ cup shortening	1 teaspoon vanilla
⅓ cup peanut butter	½ teaspoon soda
⅔ cup sugar	1½ cups Hungarian® High Altitude® Flour
1 egg	
1 teaspoon salt	

Cream together all ingredients, except flour, until fluffy. Blend in flour. Press into bottom of ungreased 13x9-inch pan.

Bake at 350° F. for 20 to 25 minutes, or until light golden brown. (Do not overbake.) Cool a few minutes; frost with Peanut Butter Frosting. (See Frosting Section.) Cut, while warm, into 2-inch squares.

CHOCOLATE PEANUT SQUARES

Add 2 ounces melted **unsweetened chocolate** and 2 tablespoons **milk** with the egg. Sprinkle batter in pan with sugar. Frost, if desired.

BROWN EYED SUSANS

Arrange 24 **solid chocolate wafers** on top of hot bars so a wafer will center each 2-inch square.

PEANUT BUTTER CHIP BARS

Add 1 cup (6 oz.) **chocolate flavored chips** with the flour.

LIGHT FRUIT CAKES

"Use any combination of nuts and fruit you desire in these moist butter cake bars."

BAKE 350° F. for 30 to 40 minutes

MAKES: 13x9-inch pan

¾ cup butter or margarine	1½ cups Hungarian® High Altitude® Flour
¾ cup sugar	
1 tablespoon grated lemon or orange peel	1 cup whole filberts or other nuts
½ teaspoon baking powder	1 cup sultana (golden) raisins
½ teaspoon salt	
3 eggs	1 cup candied cherries, halved

Cream together butter and sugar. Add lemon peel, baking powder, salt and eggs; beat well. Stir in remaining ingredients. Spread in greased 13x9-inch pan.

Bake at 350° F. for 30 to 40 minutes, or until light golden brown. Frost with Lemon or Orange Frosting. (See Frosting Section.)

ENGLISH TEACAKES

Omit nuts and fruit. Add 1 cup **currants** and 1 teaspoon **anise seed.** Sprinkle batter in pan with ½ cup **almond slices** and 3 tablespoons **sugar.** Bake. Do not frost.

MOLASSES TOFFEES

"Chewy molasses cookies with a special snap and flavor."

BAKE: 350° F. for 15 to 20 minutes

MAKES: 15x10-inch pan

¾ cup shortening	1½ cups Hungarian® High Altitude® Flour
¾ cup sugar	
¼ teaspoon soda	¾ cup coconut or chopped nuts
¼ teaspoon salt	
¼ cup light molasses	

Cream together shortening, sugar, soda, salt and molasses. Blend in flour and coconut. Spread in greased 15x10-inch pan.

Bake at 350° F. for 15 to 20 minutes. Cut into squares while warm.

LEMON CHEWSIES

"Moist and chewy bars glazed with a lemon icing."

BAKE: 360° F. for 20 to 25 minutes

MAKES: 15x10-inch pan

½ cup butter or margarine	1⅔ cups Hungarian High Altitude® Flour
1 cup packed brown sugar	
1 teaspoon salt	1 cup quick-cooking rolled oats
¼ teaspoon soda	
1 tablespoon grated lemon peel	1⅓ cups (14-oz. can) sweetened condensed milk

Cream together butter, brown sugar, salt and soda. Blend in the remaining ingredients. Spread in well-greased and floured 15x10-inch pan.

Bake at 360° F. for 20 to 25 minutes, or until light golden brown. Frost hot, with Lemon Frosting. (See Frosting Section.)

SWISS CANDY COOKIES

"Honey and a perfect blend of spices add crunch and flavor to this fruit and almond bar."

BAKE: 360° F. for 20 to 25 minutes

MAKES: 13x9-inch pan

½ cup butter or margarine	½ teaspoon cardamom, crushed
1 cup Hungarian® High Altitude® Flour	½ teaspoon cinnamon
½ cup sugar	½ cup cut candied cherries
½ teaspoon anise seed, crushed	½ cup chopped almonds
½ teaspoon coriander, crushed, if desired	¼ cup honey

Cut butter into flour, sugar and spices until particles are fine. (With mixer, use low speed.) Stir in candied cherries, almonds and honey. Spread or press with floured fingers into bottom of greased 13x9-inch pan.

Bake at 360° F. for 20 to 25 minutes, or until light golden brown. Cool 10 minutes. Cut into squares. Sprinkle with **powdered sugar.**

COCO-SCOTCH SWEETS

"Coconut, chocolate chips and condensed milk are the winning combination in these bars."

BAKE: 350° F. for 30 to 35 minutes

MAKES: 13x9-inch pan

½ cup butter or margarine	1 cup (6 oz.) chocolate or butterscotch chips
1 cup Hungarian® High Altitude® Flour	1½ cups flaked coconut
1 cup quick-cooking rolled oats	1⅓ cups (14-oz. can) sweetened condensed milk
1 teaspoon baking powder	
½ cup packed brown sugar	

Melt butter in 13x9-inch pan. Butter sides of pan. Combine the next 4 ingredients. Sprinkle evenly into pan. Top with chips, then coconut. Drizzle condensed milk evenly over mixture. (Be sure milk covers all the dry ingredients.)

Bake at 350° F. for 30 to 35 minutes, or until light golden brown.

A BAR COOKIE EXCHANGE

Do you want a variety of bars with a limited amount of baking? The fun way to do it is through a cookie exchange party. The bars can be baked at home or have someone buy the ingredients and get together to bake the cookies. Four or eight people is a good number for a bar cookie exchange. With 4 people each one can bring two pans of bar cookies (each a different kind). If 8 persons participate each should bring two pans of the same bar recipe. Divide each pan into fourths and take one of each kind. Either way you will end up with 8 different kinds of bars.

A little organization is always good. It can mean a better variety. Here's a list to choose from:

Easy Fudge Toppers	Molasses Toffees	Moravian Sugar Cookies
Austrian Butter Cookies	Sugar 'N Chip Bars	Gingersnap Chews
Butter Crunch	Peanut Meringue Bars	Molasses Crisps
Peanut Butter Candy Bars	Matrimonial (Date) Bars	Chocolate Chip Bars
Toasty Coconut Bars	Swedish Blonde Brownies	Swedish Bar Cookies

SCOTCHY PEANUT CRUNCH

"For peanut butter lovers — peanut butter in the cookie and crunch topping."

BAKE: 360° F. for 15 to 20 minutes

MAKES: 15x10-inch pan

¾ cup shortening (half butter may be used)	½ teaspoon baking powder
½ cup peanut butter	2 cups Hungarian® High Altitude® Flour
¾ cup packed brown sugar	1 cup (6 oz.) chocolate chips
1 teaspoon salt	
1 teaspoon vanilla	

Combine first 6 ingredients; beat well. Blend in flour. Press into bottom of ungreased 15x10-inch pan.

Bake at 360° F. for 15 to 20 minutes, or until light golden brown. Spread hot bars with Peanut Crunch. Sprinkle with chocolate chips. Place in hot oven 2 to 3 minutes to soften chocolate. Spread to frost.

Peanut Crunch:

Bring to a boil ½ cup **sugar** and ½ cup light **corn syrup.** Stir in 1 cup **butterscotch pieces,** ½ cup **peanut butter** and 1 cup coarsely crushed **chow mein noodles** or **rice crispy cereal.** Spread immediately.

SWEDISH BUTTER STRIPS

"Bar cookies made the Swedish way. Chocolate chips are nestled in a butter cookie — good for the family or good for company."

BAKE: 360° F. for 15 to 20 minutes

MAKES: about 4 dozen

¾ cup butter or margarine	2 cups Hungarian® High Altitude® Flour
⅔ cup sugar	½ cup chocolate chips
1 egg	½ cup chopped nuts
1 teaspoon vanilla	
½ teaspoon salt	

Cream together butter, sugar, egg, vanilla and salt. Blend in remaining ingredients. Divide dough into 4 equal parts. Shape into 12-inch rolls. Place 3 inches apart on ungreased cookie sheets. Flatten with floured fork to ¼ inch.

Bake at 360° F. for 15 to 20 minutes, or until delicately brown on edges. Cool a few minutes. Cut with sharp knife into 1-inch diagonals.

MAPLE PECAN STRIPS

Omit the chocolate chips. Use chopped **pecans** and add ½ teaspoon **maple flavor.**

SWEDISH COCONUT STRIPS

Substitute 1 cup toasted **coconut** for the chocolate chips and nuts. See Baking Aids for toasting coconut.

CHRISTMAS BUTTER STRIPS

Substitute ½ cup chopped red **candied cherries** for the chocolate chips.

SWISS CHOCOLATE STICKS

"Delicate chocolate butter bars topped with a golden coconut crunch."

BAKE: 350° F. for 15 to 20 minutes

MAKES: 40 sticks

½ cup butter or margarine	2 tablespoons cocoa
¾ cup sugar	½ teaspoon salt
1 egg	½ cup flaked coconut
1 cup Hungarian® High Altitude® Flour	

Cream butter with ½ cup sugar. Blend in egg, flour, cocoa, baking powder and salt. Spread to a 12x9-inch rectangle on foil-lined cookie sheet. Brush with water. Combine ¼ cup sugar and coconut; sprinkle over bars. Fold up sides of foil.

Bake at 350° F. for 15 to 20 minutes or until coconut is golden brown. Cut immediately into 3x1-inch strips.

EASY FUDGE TOPPERS

"These two-tone bars are delightfully delicious. An extra easy fudge topping bakes on a Swedish butter cookie."

BAKE: 375° F. for 10 minutes and 20 minutes

MAKES: 13x9-inch pan

1½ cups Hungarian® High Altitude® Flour	1⅓ cups (14-oz. can) sweetened condensed milk
¾ cup butter or margarine	1 cup (6 oz.) chocolate chips
⅓ cup powdered sugar	½ cup almond slices, other chopped nuts or coconut
½ teaspoon vanilla	
¼ teaspoon salt	

Combine flour, butter, powdered sugar, vanilla and salt in mixing bowl. Beat at low speed of mixer until particles are fine. Press into bottom of ungreased 13x9-inch pan. Bake at 375° F. for 10 minutes.

Heat condensed milk in saucepan. Stir in chocolate chips until melted and smooth. Pour over partially baked crust. Sprinkle with almonds. Bake 20 minutes. Cool; cut into small squares.

MINT CHOCOLATE CREAMS

"Delicately flavored chocolate brownies topped with fondant and a mint chocolate glaze. You'll like them as plain brownies with a chocolate frosting, too. (Omit the egg yolk.)"

BAKE: 350° F. for 25 to 35 minutes

MAKES: 9x9-inch pan

Combine in mixing bowl:

1 cup sugar	2 tablespoons cocoa
¾ cup Hungarian® High Altitude® Flour	1 egg yolk (reserve white)
⅓ cup soft butter or margarine	2 eggs
	¼ teaspoon salt

Beat at low speed 1 minute. Spread in greased 9x9, 11x7 or 10x8-inch pan.

Bake at 350° F. for 25 to 35 minutes. Cool. Frost with Fondant. Drizzle with Glaze.

Mock Fondant:

Combine 1 **egg white** with 2 to 2½ cups **powdered sugar** and ½ teaspoon **vanilla** or peppermint extract until of spreading consistency.

Mint Glaze:

Melt over hot water ½ cup **mint-flavored semi-sweet chocolate chips** and 1 tablespoon **shortening**.

LEMON GLAZERS

"Tart lemony bars that are always a refreshing touch."

BAKE: 375° F. for 20 to 25 minutes

MAKES: 13x9-inch pan

¾ cup butter or margarine
⅔ cup packed brown sugar
¼ cup cream
(sweet or sour)
½ teaspoon vanilla
¾ teaspoon soda
½ teaspoon salt
1½ cups Hungarian High Altitude® Flour
1 cup quick-cooking rolled oats

Cream together all ingredients except flour and oats. Blend in flour and oats. Spread dough in ungreased 13x9-inch pan.

Bake at 375° F. for 20 to 25 minutes, or until light golden brown. Brush immediately with Glaze.

Lemon Glaze:

Combine 1 cup **powdered sugar,** 2 tablespoons soft **butter** and 3 tablespoons **lemon juice.**

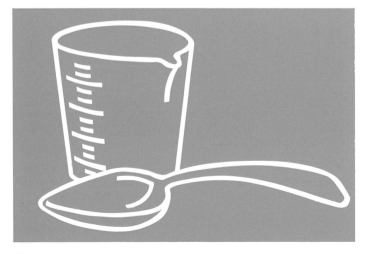

TOFFEE SQUARES

"Brown sugar-butter bars with an easy chocolate topping — you just let the chips melt on the hot bars, then spread to frost."

BAKE: 350° F. for 25 to 30 minutes

MAKES: 15x10-inch pan

1 cup butter or margarine
1 cup packed brown sugar
1 teaspoon vanilla
2 cups Hungarian High Altitude® Flour
1 cup (6 oz.) chocolate chips
1 cup chopped walnuts

Cream butter, brown sugar and vanilla. Mix in flour, ½ cup chocolate chips and ¾ cup nuts. Press into bottom of greased 15x10-inch pan.

Bake at 350° F. for 25 to 30 minutes, or until light golden brown. Immediately sprinkle with ½ cup chocolate chips. When soft, spread to frost. Sprinkle with ¼ cup nuts. Cut into squares while warm.

TOFFEE BARS

"Oatmeal, brown sugar and butter combine to make this cookie taste like a candy bar."

BAKE: 350° F. for 15 minutes and 5 minutes

MAKES: 13x9-inch pan

1 cup Hungarian High Altitude® Flour
1 cup quick-cooking rolled oats
½ cup butter or margarine
½ cup packed brown sugar
1 teaspoon baking powder
½ cup almond slices
Topping:
⅔ cup packed brown sugar
⅔ cup butter or margarine

Combine first 5 ingredients. Mix on low speed of mixer until particles are fine. Press into greased 13x9-

inch pan. Sprinkle with almond slices. Bake at 350°
F. for 15 minutes, or until light brown.

Boil together Topping ingredients 3 minutes. Pour
over partially baked base. Bake 5 minutes.

SWEDISH ALMOND CREAMS
Omit Topping. Combine in small saucepan ½ cup
sugar, ¼ cup **cream,** 1 tablespoon **flour** and ½ cup
butter or margarine; boil 2 minutes. Pour over partially baked base. Bake 5 minutes.

CARAMEL NUTTIES

*"Just like on a caramel apple. Crisp, chewy brown
sugar bars smothered with a caramel
topping and nuts."*

BAKE: 350° F. for 20 to 25 minutes

MAKES: 13x9-inch pan

½ **cup plus** ⅓ **cup butter or margarine**	½ **pound (about 28) candy caramels**
½ **cup packed brown sugar**	¼ **cup milk**
2 **cups Hungarian High Altitude Flour**	½ **cup pecans, finely chopped**
½ **teaspoon baking powder**	
1 **teaspoon vanilla**	

Melt butter in saucepan. Stir in brown sugar, flour,
baking powder and vanilla. Press into bottom of ungreased 13x9-inch pan.

Bake at 350° F. for 20 to 25 minutes, or until very light
golden. **(Do not overbake.)** Melt caramels in milk in
top of double boiler over boiling water. Spread over
cookies. Sprinkle with pecans.

SUNDAE BROWNIES

*"Chocolate syrup makes brownies taste like
a chocolate sundae. This recipe makes
lots of brownies too."*

BAKE: 350° F. for 25 to 30 minutes

MAKES: 15x10-inch pan

Combine in mixing bowl:

1¼ **cups Hungarian High Altitude Flour**	3 **eggs**
½ **cup plus** ⅓ **cup sugar**	⅔ **cup shortening**
2 **tablespoons milk**	1 **cup chocolate syrup***
1 **teaspoon salt**	¾ **cup chopped nuts, if desired**
1 **teaspoon vanilla**	

Beat at medium speed 1 minute. Spread in greased
15x10-inch pan.

Bake at 350° F. for 25 to 30 minutes. Frost warm or
cold.

Chocolate Sundae Frosting:
Combine ½ cup **chocolate syrup** (remainder of 16-
oz. can), 2 tablespoons soft **butter** or margarine, 1½
cups **powdered sugar** and ½ teaspoon **vanilla.** If necessary, add **milk** until of spreading consistency.

*It takes a 16-oz. can for the brownies and the
frosting.

SCANDINAVIAN TOSCA BARS

"A buttery bar with a delicate baked-on almond cream topping."

BAKE: 375° F. for 15 to 20 and 5 to 10 minutes

MAKES: 9x9-inch pan

½ cup butter or margarine	2 tablespoons butter or
½ cup powdered sugar	margarine
1¼ cups Hungarian® High	½ cup slivered or sliced
Altitude® Flour	almonds
½ cup sugar	1 tablespoon Hungarian®
2 tablespoons cream or	High Altitude® Flour
milk	½ teaspoon almond
	extract

Cream butter with powdered sugar. Blend in flour until particles are fine. Press into bottom of ungreased 9x9, 11x7 or 10x8-inch pan. Bake at 375° F. for 15 to 20 minutes, or until light golden brown.

Combine sugar with remaining ingredients in small saucepan. Boil 2 minutes. Pour over partially baked crust. Bake 5 to 10 minutes, or until bubbly and light golden brown. Cool; cut into squares.

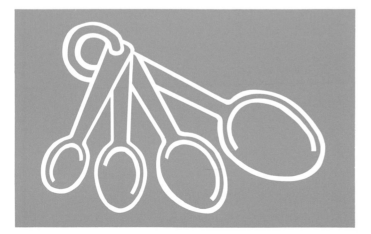

COCO-ROONS

"The refreshing combination of orange and lemon with the toasty coconut crunch makes these strips of cookies extra special."

BAKE: 350° F. for 15 to 20 minutes

MAKES: about 5 dozen

½ cup butter or margarine	1 tablespoon grated
½ cup sugar	orange peel
1 egg	1 cup plus 2 tablespoons
1 tablespoon grated	Hungarian® High
lemon peel	Altitude® Flour
	1 cup flaked or grated
	coconut

Cream together butter, sugar, egg and peels. Blend in flour. Divide into 4 equal parts. Roll each part in coconut to a 12-inch strip. Place 3 inches apart on ungreased cookie sheets.

Bake at 350° F. for 15 to 20 minutes, or until light golden brown. Cool 5 minutes; cut into 1-inch strips.

BUTTER CRUNCH

"Delectable bars that combine the flavors of butter and almonds with an easy chocolate frosting."

BAKE: 360° F. for 20 to 25 minutes

MAKES 15x10-inch pan

1 cup butter or margarine	½ teaspoon salt
1¼ cups sugar	¼ teaspoon almond
2 cups Hungarian® High	extract
Altitude® Flour	½ cup almond slices
½ teaspoon baking	
powder	

Melt butter in saucepan. Stir in remaining ingredients. Press evenly into bottom of greased 15x10-inch pan.

Bake at 360° F. for 20 to 25 minutes, or until delicate golden brown on edge. (Do not overbake.) Sprinkle immediately with 1 cup (6 oz.) **semi-sweet or milk chocolate chips.** When soft, spread to frost. Cool; break into small pieces. (Or cut into bars while warm.)

GOLDEN CANDY CHIPS

"Pieces of caramelized sugar add crunch and flavor to crisp sugar cookie bars."

BAKE: 350° F. for 15 to 20 minutes

MAKES: 4 dozen

¾ **cup and 1 tablespoon sugar**	¼ **teaspoon salt**
½ **cup butter or margarine**	1 **cup Hungarian® High Altitude® Flour**

Heat ¼ cup sugar in small skillet until melted and golden. Pour onto greased cookie sheet to harden. Crush fine. (Place between 2 sheets of waxed paper and crush with hammer.)

Soften butter with ½ cup sugar and salt. Blend in flour and crushed sugar. (Mixture may be crumbly.) Press firmly to a 12x9-inch rectangle on foil-lined cookie sheet. Fold up sides of foil. Sprinkle with 1 tablespoon sugar.

Bake at 350° F. for 15 to 20 minutes or until light golden brown. Cool 5 minutes; cut into about 1½-inch squares.

PEANUT BRITTLE CHIPS
Omit the caramelized sugar and add ⅓ cup finely crushed **peanut brittle** to the flour mixture.

CHOCOLATE-IN-OATMEAL BARS

"An easy chocolate filling hides between an oatmeal brown sugar cookie."

BAKE: 375° F. for 25 to 30 minutes

MAKES: 13x9-inch pan

¾ **cup butter or margarine**	1⅓ **cups (14-oz. can) sweetened condensed milk**
1 **cup packed brown sugar**	
½ **teaspoon salt**	
1½ **cups Hungarian® High Altitude® Flour**	1 **cup (6 oz.) chocolate chips**
1 **cup rolled oats**	½ **cup chopped nuts**

Cream butter with brown sugar and salt. Blend in flour and oats until particles are fine. Press ⅔ of crumb mixture firmly into bottom of ungreased 13x9-inch pan. Heat condensed milk in saucepan. Stir in chocolate chips and nuts. Spread over mixture in pan. Sprinkle with remaining crumbs; press down lightly.

Bake at 375° F. for 25 to 30 minutes, or until light golden brown.

BUTTERSCOTCH BETWEENS
Substitute 1 cup **butterscotch chips** for the chocolate chips.

SPICES

Nutmeg and Mace are somewhat similar in flavor and can be used interchangeably in recipes.

Cloves and Allspice: A little bit of cloves goes a long way. If you don't like the strong pungent flavor and aroma of cloves, substitute allspice. Allspice has a sweeter, spicy taste and aroma. Its flavor and aroma is sometimes said to resemble a blend of cinnamon, nutmeg and cloves.

Ginger is a must in pepparkakor and gingersnap cookies. Like several other spices, it has a real sweet, spicy flavor and a little goes a long way.

YUM YUM BARS

"Coconut, caramel sauce and milk chocolate give this attractive bar its unique flavor."

BAKE: 360° F. for 25 to 30 minutes

MAKES: 9x9-inch pan

⅓ cup butter or margarine	2 tablespoons milk
1 cup Hungarian® High Altitude® Flour	2 tablespoons flour
¼ cup packed brown sugar	2 tablespoons butter or margarine, melted
2 cups flaked coconut	¼ cup powdered sugar
½ cup caramel sundae sauce	

Cut butter into flour and sugar until particles are fine. (With mixer, use low speed.) Press into bottom of ungreased 9x9, 10x8 or 11x7-inch pan.

Combine remaining ingredients; spread carefully over crust. Bake at 360° F. for 25 to 30 minutes, or until golden brown. Cool. Drizzle with frosting. Cut into about 3x1-inch bars.

Chocolate Frosting:

Melt together ¼ cup **chocolate chips,** 1 tablespoon **butter** or margarine, 1 tablespoon **milk** and ¼ cup **powdered sugar.**

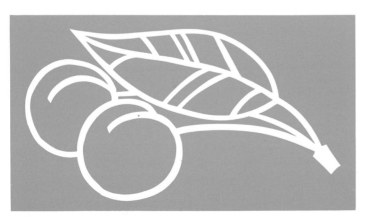

OATMEAL CRUNCH

"Sure to please the family are these crunchy brown sugar bars full of chocolate pieces and nuts."

BAKE: 360° F. for 20 to 25 minutes

MAKES: 15x10-inch pan

1 cup butter or margarine	1⅓ cups Hungarian® High Altitude® Flour
1 cup packed brown sugar	1 cup rolled oats
1 teaspoon vanilla	½ cup chopped nuts
½ teaspoon salt	½ cup chocolate chips
¼ teaspoon soda	

Cream butter with brown sugar, vanilla and salt. Stir in remaining ingredients. Press into bottom of ungreased 15x10-inch pan.

Bake at 360° F. for 20 to 25 minutes or until golden brown. Cool; cut into bars. (For a thicker bar, bake in a 13x9-inch pan 25 to 30 minutes.) For frosting, sprinkle ½ cup **chocolate chips** on hot bars. When soft, spread to frost.

FRUIT CAKE SQUARES

"A lemon frosting adds an interesting touch to these exquisite dark fruitcake bars."

BAKE: 350° F. for 40 to 50 minutes

MAKES: 13x9-inch pan

2 eggs	½ teaspoon nutmeg
1 cup sugar	¼ teaspoon ginger
½ cup shortening, melted	1½ cups Hungarian® High Altitude® Flour
½ cup milk	1 cup raisins
¼ cup light molasses	2 cups mixed candied fruit
¾ teaspoon baking powder	1 cup chopped nuts
1 teaspoon cinnamon	
½ teaspoon salt	

Combine all ingredients except flour, fruit and nuts; beat well. Stir in remaining ingredients. Spread in greased 13x9-inch pan.

Bake at 350° F. for 40 to 50 minutes. Frost warm with Lemon or Orange Frosting. (See Frosting Section.)

SWEET CRACKER COOKIES

*"Just right when you want something sweet,
but not too sweet."*

BAKE: 375° F. for 12 to 16 minutes

MAKES: 42 two-inch squares

1 cup Hungarian® High Altitude® Flour	½ teaspoon anise seed
½ cup Hungarian® High Altitude® Whole Wheat Flour	½ teaspoon salt
	½ cup soft butter or margarine
¼ cup sugar	¼ cup milk

Combine all ingredients, mixing until can form into dough. Roll out on greased cookie sheet to a 14x10-inch rectangle. Cut into 2-inch squares. Sprinkle with **sugar.** Prick with fork. Bake at 375° F. for 12 to 16 minutes, or until light golden brown. Remove cookies from edge as they brown. Continue to bake remainder.

Note: Cookie dough may be divided in half; roll each to a 10x8-inch rectangle. If your cookie sheet has sides so you can't roll out dough, use bottom of sheet.

BUTTERSCOTCH BARS

"Butterscotch (or chocolate) chips add the flavor and corn flakes the crunch to this easy cookie."

BAKE: 350° F. for 25 to 30 minutes

MAKES: 13x9-inch pan

½ cup butter or margarine	1 cup Hungarian® High Altitude® Flour
1¼ cups sugar	
2 eggs	1 cup coarsely crushed corn flakes
1 teaspoon vanilla	
½ teaspoon salt	½ cup butterscotch chips
¼ teaspoon baking powder	

Melt butter with sugar. Remove from heat. Stir in remaining ingredients except butterscotch chips. Spread in greased and floured 13x9-inch pan. Sprinkle with chips.

Bake at 350° F. for 25 to 30 minutes, or until light golden brown on edges. (Do not overbake.)

PRIZE BUTTER BARS

"Something new in bar cookies—a butterscotch-coconut filling bakes on top of butter cookies."

BAKE: 375° F. for 5 minutes and 25 to 30 minutes

MAKES: 13x9-inch pan

¾ cup butter or margarine	⅓ cup (3 oz.) cream cheese
½ cup sugar	
2 cups Hungarian® High Altitude® Flour	¼ cup butter or margarine
	¾ cup packed brown sugar
½ teaspoon vanilla	
¼ teaspoon salt	1 cup coconut or chopped nuts

Beat together the first 5 ingredients until particles are fine. (With mixer, use low speed.) Press all but 1 cup firmly into bottom of ungreased 13x9-inch pan.

Combine remaining ingredients; beat well. Spoon here and there over mixture in pan.

Bake at 375° F. for 5 minutes. Spread topping to cover. Sprinkle with remaining crumbs.

Bake 25 to 30 minutes, or until light golden brown.

Molasses: The lighter flavored molasses is generally preferred for cookie and cake baking. Use the dark molasses for quick and yeast breads when a richer caramel flavor and color is desirable.

TOFFEE TOPPERS

"Delectable bars that make a good candy."

BAKE: 375° F. for 15 to 20 minutes and 5 minutes

MAKES: 13x9-inch pan

Base:
1½ cups Hungarian® High Altitude® Flour
½ cup shortening
¼ cup brown sugar
2 tablespoons milk
¼ teaspoon soda
½ teaspoon salt
½ cup chopped nuts

Topping:
⅔ cup butter or margarine
⅔ cup packed brown sugar
¾ cup semi-sweet or milk chocolate chips

Blend together Base ingredients until particles are fine. (With mixer, use low speed.) Press firmly into bottom of greased 13x9-inch pan.

Bake at 375° F. for 15 to 20 minutes, or until golden brown. Prick generously with fork. Combine butter and brown sugar. Boil 4 minutes; mix well. Pour over base. Bake 5 minutes. Let stand 10 minutes; sprinkle with chocolate pieces. When soft, spread to frost. Cut into squares while warm.

AUSTRIAN BUTTER COOKIES

"Buttery hazelnut (filbert) cookies touched up with a tart jelly filling and a chocolate glaze. Perfect for the party tray."

BAKE: 375° F. for 20 to 25 minutes

MAKES: 13x9-inch pan

1 cup soft butter or margarine
½ cup sugar
1½ cups Hungarian® High Altitude® Flour

1 cup (3½ oz). filberts, ground or finely chopped

Blend all ingredients together until dough forms. Press into bottom of ungreased 13x9-inch pan.
Bake at 375° F. for 20 to 25 minutes, or until light golden brown. Cool. Spread with ½ cup **red jelly.** Frost.

Chocolate Glaze:

Melt together ½ cup **chocolate chips** and 1 tablespoon **shortening.**

Tip: The easy way to finely chop or grind nuts is in the electric blender; it takes only seconds.

PENUCHE TREASURES

"A butterscotch brownie bakes on top of a coconut-brown sugar mixture."

BAKE: 375° F. for 20 to 25 minutes

MAKES: 13x9-inch pan

½ cup and 2 tablespoons butter or margarine
1 cup flaked coconut
1⅓ cups packed brown sugar
2 eggs

1 cup Hungarian® High Altitude® Flour
¾ teaspoon baking powder
1 teaspoon vanilla
½ teaspoon salt

Melt 2 tablespoons butter in 13x9-inch pan; spread in pan. Sprinkle with coconut and ⅓ cup brown sugar. Melt ½ cup butter and 1 cup brown sugar in 2-quart saucepan. Stir in remaining ingredients. Pour over coconut mixture.

Bake at 375° F. for 20 to 25 minutes. Cool. If desired, frost with Praline Frosting. (See Praline Candy Bars.) (Leave bars in pan.)

CARAMEL MACAROON BARS

"A macaroon filling bakes atop a caramel base."

BAKE: 360° F. for 20 minutes and 25 to 30 minutes

MAKES: 9x9-inch pan

¼ cup butter or margarine, melted	1 egg
¾ cup packed brown sugar	2 cups grated cookie or flaked coconut
½ cup Hungarian® High Altitude® Flour	1⅓ cups (14-oz. can) sweetened condensed milk
¼ teaspoon baking powder	

Combine first 5 ingredients; blend well. Spread in greased 9x9, 10x8 or 11x7-inch pan. Bake at 360° F. for 20 minutes. Combine coconut and milk. Spoon over caramel base. Spread to cover. Bake 25 to 30 minutes, or until light golden brown. Cool and frost. Cut into small squares.

Caramel Frosting:
Melt 2 tablespoons **butter** or margarine and 2 tablespoons **milk** with ¼ cup **brown sugar**. Stir in 1 cup **powered sugar**.

SPANISH BUTTER "STIX"

"These crisp, crunchy butter cookies are of peanuts. You can make them a double treat for the youngsters by using half chocolate chips. Or try something like sunflower or soya nuts."

BAKE: 350° F. for 20 to 25 minutes

MAKES: about 5 dozen

¾ cup sugar	2 cups Hungarian® High Altitude® Flour
1 cup soft butter or margarine	1 cup Spanish salted peanuts
½ teaspoon baking powder	

Cream together sugar, butter and baking powder. Blend in flour until dough forms. Stir in peanuts. Divide into 5 equal parts. Shape into 12-inch rolls. Place at least 3 inches apart on ungreased cookie sheets. Flatten with floured fork to ¼ inch.

Bake at 350° F. for 20 to 25 minutes, or until light golden brown on edges. Cool a few minutes. Cut with sharp knife into 1-inch diagonals.

BROWN SUGAR
Light brown sugar was used in all the recipes in this book. If you use dark brown sugar, the product may brown faster. Dark brown sugar gives a very rich, heavy and almost molasses-like caramel flavor. Cookies made with the dark sugar will spread more than when light brown sugar is used.

S'MORE BARS

"Brown sugar bars are topped with chocolate pieces and marshmallows."

BAKE: 350° F. for 25 minutes

MAKES: 13x9-inch pan

1⅔ cups Hungarian® High Altitude® Flour	2 tablespoons milk
1¼ cups packed brown sugar	¾ teaspoon baking powder
1 egg	¼ teaspoon salt
½ cup butter or margarine	

Blend together all ingredients until dough forms. Spread in greased 13x9-inch pan.

Bake at 350° F. for 15 minutes.

Sprinkle with ½ cup **chocolate chips** and 2 cups **miniature marshmallows.** Bake 10 minutes. Melt ½ cup **chocolate chips** with 1 tablespoon **shortening.** Drizzle over marshmallows.

Test Kitchen Suggestion: The easy way to melt chocolate chips is to place them in a small custard cup with the shortening, then set cup in pan of water and heat.

PEANUT BUTTER STRIPS

"Peanut butter bars with an easy butterscotch icing."

BAKE: 360° F. for 20 to 25 minutes

MAKES: 13x9-inch pan

⅔ cup shortening	1 cup quick-cooking rolled oats
½ cup peanut butter	
1 cup sugar	1 cup (6 oz.) butterscotch chips*
1 egg	
½ teaspoon salt	¼ cup chopped salted peanuts
¼ teaspoon soda	
1 cup Hungarian® High Altitude® Flour	

Cream together first 6 ingredients. Blend in flour and oats. Press into bottom of ungreased 13x9-inch pan.

Bake at 360° F. for 20 to 25 minutes, or until very lightly browned.

Sprinkle immediately with butterscotch chips. When soft, spread to frost. Sprinkle with peanuts.

*Using half chocolate chips makes an interesting frosting. Spread carefully for a reveled appearance.

BLONDE CHIPPERS

"Oatmeal gives a different flavor and crunch to blonde brownies."

BAKE: 350° F. for 25 to 30 minutes

MAKES: 13x9-inch pan

1⅓ cups packed brown sugar	1 cup quick-cooking
½ cup shortening	rolled oats
2 eggs	1 cup Hungarian® High
⅓ cup milk	Altitude® Flour
¼ teaspoon baking powder	½ to 1 cup chocolate
½ teaspoon salt	chips

Combine all ingredients except chocolate chips in mixing bowl. Mix on low speed 1 minute. Stir in chips. Spread in greased 13x9-inch pan.

Bake at 350° F. for 25 to 30 minutes, or until golden brown. If desired, frost with Praline Frosting. (See Praline Candy Bars Page 54)

LUSCIOUS TEA BARS

"Brown sugar moist and chewy with coconut and chocolate pieces are these unusual bars."

BAKE: 375° F. for 25 to 30 minutes

MAKES: 15x10-inch pan

½ cup butter or margarine	1 cup Hungarian® High
1 cup packed brown sugar	Altitude® Flour
1 cup half & half cream	¾ teaspoon baking
2 cups graham cracker	powder
crumbs	2 cups flaked coconut
	1 cup chocolate chips

Cream together butter and brown sugar. Stir in remaining ingredients. Spread in greased and floured 15x10-inch pan.

Bake at 375° F. for 25 to 30 minutes, or until light golden brown.

CONVERSIONS TO METRIC MEASURES FOR RECIPES (APPROXIMATE)

WHEN YOU KNOW:	YOU CAN FIND THE:	IF YOU MULTIPLY U.S. MEASURE BY	OR VICE VERSA MULTIPLY METRIC BY:
teaspoons (tsp)	milliliters (ml)	5	.20
Tablespoons (Tbsp)	milliliters (ml)	15	.067
fluid ounces (fl oz)	milliliters (ml)	30	.033
dry ounces (oz)	grams (g)	28	.036
pounds (lb)	kilograms (kg)	0.45	2.2
cups (c)	liters (l)	0.24	4.16
pints (pt)	liters (l)	0.47	2.13
quarts (qt)	liters (l)	0.95	1.05
gallons (gal)	liters (l)	3.8	.26
degrees fahr. (°F)	degrees centrigrade (°c)	subtract 32 & multiply by 5/9	multiply by 9/5 & add 32

BAKING AIDS & QUICK TRICKS

MEASURING:

All measurements are level. Standard measuring cups and spoons have been used. Using heaping measurement or poor measuring equipment could cause baking failures.

ELECTRIC MIXER:

Bake the easy way, using Hungarian® High Altitude® flour Kitchen tested recipes. Let your mixer work for you. Keep it on the kitchen counter so it will be ready to use. Use it for combining ingredients, beating, creaming, blending, mixing, stirring and cutting. Lowest speed is best for stirring and cutting shortenings into dry ingredients. Scrape the sides of the bowl occasionally for good blending.

PAN SIZES:

For correct pan size measure top inside length and width, if pan size is not given on bottom. Using a small pan will give a thicker, more "cake-like" bar and require a longer baking time. A larger pan makes a thinner, crisper bar requiring a shorter baking time.
9x9 almost equals 10x8 and 11x7-inch pans
8x8 equals a 9-inch round pan
13x9 equals two 8x8-inch pans

MINUTE MINDERS:

Preheat the oven. Be sure it has reached the correct temperature before you place product in oven.
While baking, check product at minimum suggested

time, then bake longer as needed. If two pan sizes are suggested in a recipe, the larger pan will bake a shorter time while the smaller pan will require a longer baking time. Because oven temperatures do vary, it is possible you may need to bake the recipe a longer or shorter time than recommended.

Baking temperatures and times are developed for aluminum and stainless steel pans. If using a glass pan, lower the oven temperature 25° F.

QUICK TRICKS IN BAKING:

● Use a French knife for chopping nuts, fruit and raisins. Grease knife or coat fruit and raisins with one tablespoon of the flour to prevent sticking. Chopped raisins are easier to cut through in a bar cookie and cake.

● Drain maraschino cherries and other moist fruit thoroughly on paper toweling.

● When toasting coconut or almonds, place in 375° F. oven for 5 to 8 minutes until golden brown; stir occasionally for even browning.

● Use kitchen scissors to cut dates, figs and marsh-mallows. Dip in hot water if there is sticking.

● When dusting bars with powdered sugar, tap or press it through a sieve — this removes lumps and coats evenly.

● An easy frosting for brownies and other bars is to sprinkle with chocolate chips as soon as removed from the oven; let stand a few minutes and spread to frost. Do not return to oven, this just dries out the chips. A couple tablespoons peanut butter adds a nice flavor.

● When rolling or pressing out dough on cookie sheet, place sheet on wet paper towel or cloth to prevent slipping.

ALTITUDE ADJUSTMENTS

All the recipes in this book have been tested with Hungarian®High Altitude®Flour at an altitude of 5200 feet above sea level. If you live at an altitude of more than 5500 feet above sea level you may find it necessary to decrease the leavening ⅛, ¼ or even as much as ½ teaspoon at 6500 feet or higher. Decreasing the sugar 1 or 2 tablespoons and/or increasing the flour 1 or 2 tablespoons may give better results. The products may take longer to bake or increase the baking temperature 10 to 15° F.

At 4000 feet to sea level, recipes with leavening (baking powder and soda) may need an extra ¼ teaspoon. In cake-type bars decreasing the flour 1 or 2 tablespoons may give better results. Some of the recipes will bake faster than the recommended time. If they brown too fast decrease the baking temperature 10 to 15° F.

COOKIE JAR FAVORITES

Do you ever say to yourself, "I'd like to bake more cookies for those kiddies of mine, but I just don't have the time." Well, you need not say that anymore, because all of their favorite cookie jar cookies — chocolate chip, oatmeal, salted peanut, sugar, peanut butter, and molasses — have now been made into bar cookies. They are so easy the youngsters can even make them. The taste is the same, the difference is in the shape.

SHORTBREAD

"Try some of the new flavor variations for the old-time Scotch butter cookie."

BAKE: 375° F. for 20 to 25 minutes

MAKES: about 3 dozen

2 cups Hungarian®High Altitude®Flour	¾ cup soft butter or margarine
½ cup sugar	2 tablespoons cream
	1 teaspoon vanilla

Combine all ingredients in mixing bowl. Mix until a dough can be formed. (With mixer, use a low speed.) Form into a square. Flatten on greased cookie sheet to a 10x8-inch rectangle. Prick with fork to make 2-inch triangles or squares. Do not separate.

Bake at 375° F. for 20 to 25 minutes, or until golden brown on edges. Cut along prick lines.

COFFEE SHORTBREAD

Add 2 teaspoons **instant coffee** and ¼ cup finely chopped **pecans.**

ALMOND SHORTBREAD

Add ⅓ cup **almond slices** and ½ teaspoon **almond extract.**

ORANGE PECAN SHORTBREAD

Add 2 tablespoons grated **orange peel** and ½ cup finely chopped **pecans** to dry ingredients. Frost top and sides of baked cookies with Orange Frosting, (See Frosting Section.)

LEMON COCONUT SHORTBREAD

Add 2 tablespoons grated **lemon peel** and 1 cup **cookie** or **flaked coconut** to the dry ingredients.

"SPRITZ" STIX

"The fun way to make special cookies.
Look and taste just like spritz, but you don't
need a cookie press."
BAKE: 350° F. for 15 to 20 minutes
MAKES: 72 bars

1 cup butter or margarine	¼ teaspoon salt
¾ cup sugar	2⅓ cups Hungarian® High
1 egg	Altitude® Flour
2 teaspoons vanilla	

Cream together all ingredients except flour. Blend in flour. Divide dough in half. Spread each half with floured fingers or spatula to a 12x10-inch rectangle on ungreased cookie sheet. Run floured fork tines over top to make "spritz" marks. Sprinkle with **colored sugars,** if desired.

Bake at 350° F. for 15 to 20 minutes, or until delicately browned. Cut immediately into 3x1-inch sticks. Remove from cookie sheet.

CHOCOLATE "SPRITZ"

Increase sugar to 1 cup and add 2 ounces melted **unsweetened chocolate.** Do not overbake.

BUTTERSCOTCH "SPRITZ"

Substitute **brown sugar** for the white.

ORANGE PECAN "SPRITZ"

Add 2 tablespoons grated **orange peel** and ½ cup very finely chopped **pecans** with flour.

SWEDISH SPICE "SPRITZ"

Add 1 teaspoon **cinnamon,** ¼ teaspoon **nutmeg** and ¼ teaspoon **cardamom** in first step.

COFFEE "SPRITZ"

Add 1 tablespoon **instant coffee** and ¼ cup finely chopped **pecans,** if desired, with sugar.

PEPPERKAKOR "SPRITZ"

Omit egg; add ¼ cup light **molasses** and ½ teaspoon each: **cinnamon, nutmeg, cloves** and **ginger** with sugar.

PASTEL PARTY "SPRITZ"

Add ⅛ teaspoon **food coloring** with sugar. After marking with fork tines, sprinkle with **colored sugar** (the same color as the dough).

OLD FASHIONED OATMEAL BARS

"Kids will love these soft, moist raisin spice bars.
Good with a glass of milk."
BAKE: 375° F. for 20 to 25 minutes
MAKES: 13x9-inch pan

1 cup raisins (chopped or whole)*	1 egg
¾ cup water	1 teaspoon salt
1 cup quick-cooking rolled oats	1 teaspoon cinnamon
	1 teaspoon vanilla
1 cup Hungarian® High Altitude® Flour	½ teaspoon soda
	¼ teaspoon nutmeg
⅓ cup shortening	¼ teaspoon cloves
½ cup sugar	½ cup chopped nuts, if desired

Combine raisins with water; simmer 10 minutes. Combine oats with raisins and liquid. Add remaining ingredients. Blend, then beat at medium speed 1 minute. Spread evenly in greased 13x9-inch pan.

Bake at 375° F. for 20 to 25 minutes, or until top springs back when touched lightly in center.

*Chopped raisins make bars easier to cut.

SWEDISH BUTTER BARS

"Always a popular cookie — choose from one of the 7 flavor variations."

BAKE: 375° F. for 25 to 30 minutes

MAKES: 13x9-inch pan

1 cup butter or margarine	2 cups Hungarian® High Altitude® Flour
⅔ cup powdered sugar	
1 egg	½ teaspoon salt
1 teaspoon vanilla	¾ cup chopped pecans

Cream butter with sugar, egg and vanilla. Blend in remaining ingredients. Spread in greased 13x9-inch pan.

Bake at 375° F. for 25 to 30 minutes, or until light golden brown. Sprinkle with **powdered sugar.** Cool 5 minutes. Cut into 1½-inch squares.

HAWAIIAN BUTTER BARS

Omit pecans. Add ½ cup **coconut** and ½ cup cut **candied pineapple** with the flour.

CHERRY NUT BARS

Add ½ cup cut candied or **maraschino cherries** with the flour. Frost with Chocolate Frosting. (See Frosting Section.)

CHRISTMAS BUTTER BARS

Add 1 cup mixed **candied fruit** with the flour.

CHINESE BUTTER BARS

Omit pecans. Add ½ cup chopped **almonds** and 2 tablespoons finely chopped **candied ginger** with the flour.

MEXICAN BUTTER BARS

Decrease pecans to ½ cup and add ½ cup **chocolate chips** with the flour.

TOASTY COCONUT SWEDISH BARS

Omit pecans. Add 1 cup **toasted coconut** with the flour.

TOUCH O' GOLD BARS

Add 2 tablespoons grated **orange peel** with the flour. Frost with Orange Frosting. (See Frosting Section.)

BUTTER PECAN JEWELS

"Bits of jelly nestled in a crunchy pecan topping add sparkle to this popular butter cookie."

BAKE: 375° F. for 25 to 30 minutes

MAKES: 9x9-inch pan (36 cookies)

¾ cup butter or margarine	1½ cups Hungarian® High Altitude® Flour
½ cup packed brown sugar	
¼ cup powdered sugar	1 teaspoon vanilla
1 egg (reserve 1 tablespoon white for topping)	½ teaspoon salt
	½ cup finely chopped pecans

Cream butter with sugars. Blend in egg, flour, vanilla, salt and ¼ cup pecans. Press into bottom of ungreased 9x9, 10x8 or 11x7-inch pan. Brush with reserved egg white; sprinkle with remaining pecans. Press deep holes in rows with floured finger, 1 inch apart.

Bake at 375° F. for 25 to 30 minutes, or until golden brown. (With knife handle, remark holes after 20 minutes of baking.) Immediately fill indentations with jelly, jam, chocolate chips or colored powdered sugar icing. (Swirl chips when soft.) Cool; cut into squares.

EASY IDEA

When sprinkling bars and other baked products with powdered sugar, press or tap through a sieve — it removes lumps and coats evenly.

SPANISH PEANUT BARS

"Crunchy peanut bars are sure to please the youngsters."

BAKE: 375° F. for 20 to 25 minutes

MAKES: 13x9-inch pan

¾ cup shortening	1 cup Hungarian® High
1 cup packed brown sugar	Altitude® Flour
1 egg	2 cups corn flakes
½ teaspoon salt	1½ cups Spanish salted
¼ teaspoon soda	peanuts

Combine the first 6 ingredients in mixing bowl; beat well. Stir in remaining ingredients. Spread in greased 13x9-inch pan.

Baked at 375° F. for 20 to 25 minutes, or until light golden brown. (Do not overbake.) Cut into bars while warm.

Note: For a thinner bar, spread in greased 15x10-inch pan. Bake 15 to 20 minutes.

SPANISH CHIP BARS

Decrease peanuts to 1 cup and add 1 cup **chocolate chips.**

PAN SUGGESTION

If you don't have a 15x10-inch pan, make one from heavy duty foil. Place on a cookie sheet. Fold and pinch corners tightly so the pan will hold its shape.

SUGAR SQUARES

"Sugar cookies that may be served plain, sprinkled with fancy sugar or frosted with colored icing."

BAKE: 360° F. for 25 to 30 minutes

MAKES: 13x9-inch pan

Combine in mixing bowl:

1½ cups Hungarian® High	2 tablespoons orange
Altitude® Flour	juice
½ cup sugar	1 egg
½ cup soft butter or	¾ teaspoon baking
margarine	powder
1 teaspoon grated orange	½ teaspoon salt
peel	2 teaspoons vanilla

Beat at medium speed until well blended, about 1 minute. Spread in a greased 13x9-inch pan. Sprinkle with **sugar.**

Bake at 360° F. for 25 to 30 minutes, or until light golden brown. Cool 5 minutes. Cut into squares, diamonds or rectangles.

CHOCOLATE CHIP BARS

"The all-time favorite cookie made easy for you."

BAKE: 375° F. for 15 to 20 minutes

MAKES: 13x9-inch pan

½ cup butter or margarine	1 teaspoon vanilla
⅓ cup sugar	½ teaspoon soda
⅓ cup packed brown sugar	½ teaspoon salt
1 egg	½ cup chocolate chips
1 cup Hungarian® High	½ cup chopped nuts
Altitude® Flour	

Soften butter with sugars. Add remaining ingredients; blend well. Spread in greased 13x9-inch pan. Bake at 375° F. for 15 to 20 minutes, or until light golden brown.

MORAVIAN SUGAR COOKIES

"Crisp and chewy sugar cookies with a golden coating of cinnamon sugar."

BAKE: 360° F. for 12 to 15 minutes

MAKES: 40

½ cup butter or margarine	Topping:
1 cup sugar	¼ cup sugar
½ teaspoon baking power	¼ cup finely chopped nuts
1 teaspoon vanilla	
¼ teaspoon salt	2 teaspoons cinnamon
1 egg	
1⅓ cups Hungarian®High Altitude®Flour	

Soften butter with sugar, baking powder, vanilla, salt and egg. Blend in flour. Spread half of dough on well-greased cookie sheet to 10x8-inch rectangle; smooth edges. Combine Topping ingredients; sprinkle half over dough. Repeat with remaining dough.
Bake at 360° F. for 12 to 15 minutes, or until golden brown on edges. Cool 2 minutes. Cut into 2-inch squares; remove immediately.

Hint: If cookies cool before you have cut and removed them from cookie sheet, reheat in oven a couple minutes.

Ice Cream Cookie Sandwiches
Cut the baked **Moravian Sugar Cookies** (Molasses Crisps or Old-Fashioned Sugar Cookies) into 3x2-inch rectangles. Cut **ice cream** into 3x2x½-inch rectangles. Sandwich ice cream between 2 cookies. Freeze until serving time.

GINGERSNAP CHEWS

"Tastes just like a gingersnap—and a snap to make."

BAKE: 360° F. for 20 to 25 minutes

MAKES: 13x9-inch pan

Combine in mixing bowl:

1½ cups Hungarian®High Altitude®Flour	¾ teaspoon soda
¾ cup sugar	½ teaspoon salt
½ cup shortening	½ teaspoon cinnamon
1 egg	¼ teaspoon ginger
3 tablespoons light molasses	¼ teaspoon cloves

Blend together until dough forms. Press into bottom of greased 13x9-inch pan. Brush with **water;** sprinkle with **sugar.**

Bake at 360° F. for 20 to 25 minutes. Cool; cut into squares.

HONEY SPICE CHEWS

Use **honey** instead of molasses. Add ¼ teaspoon **cardamom,** if desired.

BROWN SUGAR CHEWS

Substitute **brown sugar** for white sugar and **light corn syrup** for molasses. Add 1 teaspoon **anise seed.**

GINGERSNAP STRIPS

"Tastes just like they should. All that is different is the shape. Make them in minutes."

BAKE: 375° F. for 10 to 15 minutes

MAKES: About 6 dozen

¾ cup shortening	½ teaspoon cinnamon
1 cup sugar	¼ teaspoon ginger
1 egg	¼ teaspoon cloves
¼ cup light molasses	2 cups Hungarian® High
1½ teaspoons soda	Altitude® Flour
½ teaspoon salt	

Combine all ingredients in mixing bowl. Blend until dough forms. Divide into 6 equal parts. Shape into 12-inch rolls. Place at least 3 inches apart on greased cookie sheets. Brush tops with water; sprinkle with **sugar.** Bake at 375° F. for 10 to 15 minutes, or until golden brown. Cool 5 minutes; cut diagonally into 1-inch bars.

HONEY SPICE SNAPS
Substitute ¼ cup **honey** for molasses and ¼ teaspoon **nutmeg** for cloves. Increase **flour** to 2¼ cups.

BROWN SUGAR SNAPS
Substitute **brown sugar** and **light corn syrup** for sugar and molasses and 1½ teaspoons **anise seed** for spices. Increase **flour** to 2¼ cups.

CHEWY OATMEAL BARS

"Another favorite made easy as a bar cookie. Coconut adds chewiness and flavor."

BAKE: 375° F. for 20 to 25 minutes

MAKES: 13x9-inch pan

½ cup shortening	¾ cup Hungarian® High
1 cup packed brown sugar	Altitude® Flour
1 egg	1½ cups quick-cooking
¾ teaspoon baking powder	rolled oats
1 teaspoon salt	½ cup chopped nuts
1 teaspoon vanilla	½ cup coconut, if desired
½ teaspoon soda	

Cream together the first 8 ingredients until fluffy. Blend in remaining ingredients. Spread in greased 13x9-inch pan. Bake at 375° F. for 20 to 25 minutes. Cool 15 minutes; cut in bars.

SWEDISH TEA CAKES

"The new way to shape the most popular Christmas and party cookie."

BAKE: 350° F. for 25 to 30 minutes

MAKES: 4½ dozen

1 cup butter or margarine	2 cups Hungarian® High
½ cup powdered sugar	Altitude® Flour
2 teaspoons vanilla	1 cup finely chopped
½ teaspoon salt	pecans or other nuts

Cream butter with powdered sugar, vanilla and salt until fluffy. Blend in flour and pecans. Flatten on ungreased cookie sheet to a 9x6-inch rectangle. Cut into 1-inch squares. Do not separate.

Bake at 350° F. for 25 to 30 minutes, or until lightly browned on edges. Recut into squares. Cool 5 minutes; roll in **powdered sugar.**

MOLASSES CRISPS

"Snappy thin cookies with just the right blend of spices and molasses."

BAKE: 350° F. for 10 to 15 minutes

MAKES: 5 to 6 dozen

½ cup shortening	1 egg
⅓ cup molasses	½ teaspoon each: salt,
½ cup sugar	soda, cinnamon,
2 cups Hungarian® High	cloves, ginger, nutmeg
Altitude® Flour	

Melt shortening with molasses and sugar in saucepan. Stir in remaining ingredients. Cool, if needed. Roll out dough, half at a time, on greased cookie sheet to about a 14x10-inch rectangle; smooth edges. Sprinkle with **sugar.**

Bake at 350° F. for 10 to 15 minutes. Cut immediately into squares, diamonds or triangles. If desired, frost with Vanilla Frosting. (See Frosting Section.)

Tip: to cut **diamonds,** make horizontal cuts 2 inches apart and diagonal cuts 2 inches apart. For **triangles,** make diagonal cuts in the other direction, or cut diamonds in half.

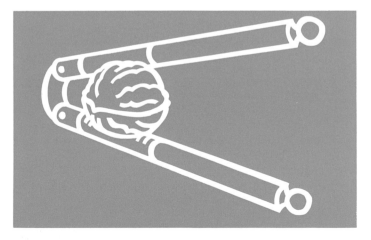

NORWEGIAN ALMOND BARS

"A rich almond filling is layered between a butter cookie mixture—so typical of Scandinavian cooking."

BAKE: 375° F. for 30 to 35 minutes

MAKES: 9x9-inch pan

1½ cups Hungarian® High	¾ cup butter or
Altitude® Flour	margarine
¼ cup sugar	1 egg
¼ teaspoon salt	1 cup almonds, ground
½ teaspoon almond extract,	1 cup powdered sugar
if desired	1 tablespoon water

Combine flour, sugar, salt, almond extract, butter and egg yolk. Mix until particles are fine using low speed of mixer. Remove ½ cup. Press remainder into bottom of ungreased 9x9-inch pan.

Combine almonds, powdered sugar, egg white and water to make a paste. Spoon over crust; spread carefully. Crumble reserved mixture over almonds.

Bake at 375° F. for 30 to 35 minutes, or until golden brown.

Short-cut Idea: Almonds can be ground or very finely chopped in an electric blender; it takes only seconds.

RAISIN PRIZE BARS

"Chewy oatmeal and raisin bars that require a little extra work to grind raisins and oatmeal, but they are worth it."

BAKE: 375° F. for 20 to 25 minutes

MAKES: 13x9-inch pan

⅔ cup shortening	1⅓ cups Hungarian® High
1 cup sugar	Altitude® Flour
½ teaspoon soda	1 cup rolled oats, ground
½ teaspoon salt	1 cup raisins, ground
1 egg	½ cup chopped nuts

Cream together shortening, sugar, soda, salt and egg. Blend in remaining ingredients. (Mixture may be crumbly.) Press firmly into bottom of greased 13x9-inch pan.

Bake at 375° F. for 20 to 25 minutes, or until very light golden brown. While warm, cut into squares.

Note: For thinner bars, bake in greased 15x10-inch pan 15 to 20 minutes.

PEANUT BUTTER STICKS

"Keep the cookie jar full of these for the youngsters. Idea—add ½ cup chocolate chips with the flour."

BAKE: 350° F. for 15 to 20 minutes

MAKES: 5 dozen

½ cup shortening	¾ teaspoon soda
½ cup peanut butter	1 teaspoon salt
½ cup sugar	1 teaspoon vanilla
½ cup packed brown sugar	2 cups plus 2 table-
1 egg	spoons Hungarian®
2 tablespoons milk	High Altitude®Flour

Beat together all ingredients except flour until fluffy. Blend in flour. Divide into 5 parts. Shape into 1-inch rolls. Place on ungreased cookie sheet, 3 inches apart. Flatten, crisscross fashion, with fork to ¼ inch.

Bake at 350° F. for 15 to 20 minutes, or until golden brown. Cool a couple of minutes; cut diagonally into 1-inch sticks.

MIXING AND BAKING TERMS:

All the recipes in this cookbook have been tested and retested and streamlined to make them quick and easy to make. With the exception of those recipes mixed up in the saucepan, use the electric mixer for the easiest and best mixing. The following terms are used throughout this book and the descriptions given below can help you in preparing the recipes. The recommended speed for the electric mixer is also noted.

Beat: To mix together briskly. For cookie and cake batters use a medium speed (3, 4, or 5) on the mixer.

Blend: To mix two or more ingredients thoroughly, or until smooth and of uniform texture and color. Sometimes it may be adding one or more ingredients to a batter or dough. Use a low speed of the mixer.

Cream: To beat a mixture until light and fluffy. Butter and other solid shortenings are often creamed with sugar(s). Use a medium or high speed on the mixer.

Cut: To mix butter or other solid shortenings with dry ingredients with the least amount of mixing or blending. It can be done with lowest speed of the mixer or with a pastry blender. The shortening should be evenly distributed in the dry ingredients and the particles fine in appearance.

Mix: To combine two or more ingredients by stirring or blending. With mixer, use low speed.

Boil: To cook a mixture at a temperature at which bubbles come to the surface continuously and break.

Caramelize: To melt sugar slowly in a heavy skillet until it becomes brown in color. The darker the color, the stronger the caramel flavor. For a caramelized sugar, pour the melted sugar onto a greased pan and let harden. For a caramel syrup, add a small amount of hot water or milk, starting with a very few drops at a time. Stir until smooth and melted.

Simmer: To cook a mixture slowly at or just below boiling point. Tiny bubbles will slowly rise to the surface (especially around the edge) and break.

SWEET SHOPPE FAVORITES

Candy-like cookies delight the recipe collector. Include a few of these on the cookie tray and you'll find they are the first to disappear. Bars in this section make good gifts. Make a box for a friend to say "thanks" for a special favor. Or a box of these bars would really please the college student. Some are old favorites, but many will be new recipes to you.

COOKIE CRUNCHIES

"Rice crispy cereal, corn flakes and peanuts are the make-up of this crunchy bar."

MAKES: 13x9-inch pan

½ cup butter or margarine	⅓ cup half & half cream
1 cup sugar	3 cups corn flakes
½ cup Hungarian® High Altitude® Flour	3 cups rice crispy cereal
½ cup light corn syrup	1 cup coconut, if desired
	1 cup salted peanuts

Combine in saucepan butter, sugar, flour, syrup and cream. Bring to a **full** boil, stirring occasionally. Boil 5 minutes. Stir in remaining ingredients. Spread in buttered 13x9-inch pan. Chill until firm.

CHOCO-PEANUT CRUNCHIES

"Peanuts in a creamy chocolate fondant top a crunchy cookie."

BAKE: 375° F. for 15 to 20 minutes

MAKES: 9x9-inch pan

Base:	Topping:
1 cup Hungarian® High Altitude® Flour	1 cup (6 oz.) chocolate chips
½ cup quick-cooking rolled oats	2 tablespoons shortening
½ cup butter or margarine	¼ cup light corn syrup
¼ cup brown sugar	¼ cup peanut butter
	1 cup Spanish salted peanuts

Mix together base ingredients until particles are fine. (With mixer, use low speed.) Press into greased 9x9, 11x7 or 10x8-inch pan. Bake at 375° F. for 15 to 20 minutes, or until light golden brown.

Melt chocolate chips with shortening and syrup in saucepan. Stir in peanut butter and peanuts. Spread over baked crust.

CHOCOLATE SNACKER BARS

"Chocolate meringue coats toasty nuts — an easy and fun holiday snack."

BAKE: 325° F. for 20 minutes and 30 to 35 minutes

MAKES: 13x9-inch pan

½ cup butter or margarine	2 egg whites
2½ cups nuts (walnut halves, almonds or other nuts)*	1 teaspoon vanilla
	1 cup sugar
½ teaspoon salt	⅔ cup Hungarian® High Altitude® Flour
½ cup chocolate chips	

Combine butter, nuts and salt in 13x9-inch pan. Toast in 325° F. oven 20 minutes; stir once. Melt chocolate chips over hot water.

Beat egg whites and vanilla until foamy. Add sugar gradually, beating until stiff. Fold in flour, then the nut mixture and melted chocolate, using as few strokes as possible. Spread in the 13x9-inch pan.

Bake at 325° F. for 30 to 35 minutes. Loosen edges and turn out onto cookie sheet. Cool. To serve, break into pieces.

*If salted peanuts are used, decrease salt to ¼ teaspoon.

Tip: An easy way to melt chocolate chips is to place them in a small custard cup. Set cup in pan of water to heat.

BUTTER CREAM BARS

"A must for the party tray — a creamy white almond bark tops a butter cookie base."

BAKE: 375° F. for 15 to 18 minutes

MAKES: 9x9-inch pan

Crust:	Topping:
½ cup soft butter or margarine	¼ cup light cream
¼ cup brown or granulated sugar	¼ cup sugar
	¼ cup butter
1¼ cups Hungarian® High Altitude® Flour	⅛ teaspoon salt
	1½ cups powdered sugar
1 tablespoon cream	½ cup unblanched or toasted almonds
½ teaspoon vanilla	½ teaspoon almond extract

Cream butter and sugar. Mix in remaining crust ingredients until particles are fine. Press into bottom of ungreased 9x9, 10x8 or 11x7-inch pan. Bake at 375° F. for 15 to 18 minutes, or until golden brown.

Boil cream, sugar, butter and salt together 4 minutes. Remove from heat. Add powdered sugar; beat until smooth. Stir in almonds and extract. Spread over baked crust.

COFFEE ALMOND BARK BARS

Add 1 teaspoon **instant coffee** to cream mixture before boiling.

CHRISTMAS ALMOND BARK

Add ½ cup **candied cherries** with the almonds.

PRALINE CREAMS

Boil together 5 minutes ¼ cup **milk**, ½ cup **brown sugar** and ¼ cup **butter** or margarine. Add 2 cups **powdered sugar**; beat until smooth. Stir in ¾ cup broken **pecans** and ½ teaspoon **vanilla**. Substitute for Topping in recipe.

CHOCOLATE SURPRISES

"The surprise? A layer of caramel and raisins hidden under the chocolate frosting."

BAKE: 375° F. for 15 to 20 minutes

MAKES: 9x9-inch pan

½ cup butter or margarine	¼ cup cream or milk
⅓ cup sugar	1 cup powdered sugar
1¼ cups Hungarian® High Altitude® Flour	1 cup raisins
½ pound (about 28) candy caramels	

Soften butter with sugar. Blend in flour until particles are fine. (With mixer, use low speed.) Press into bottom of ungreased 9x9, 10x8 or 11x7-inch pan. Bake at 375° F. for 15 to 20 minutes, or until golden brown.

Melt caramels with cream over boiling water. Stir in powdered sugar. Spread over baked crust. Top with raisins; press down slightly. Frost. Let harden; cut into bars.

Chocolate Glaze:
Melt 2 tablespoons **butter** or margarine with 2 tablespoons **milk** and ½ cup **chocolate chips.** Stir in ½ cup **powdered sugar.** Beat until smooth.

TAFFY CHEWS

"A milk chocolate icing complements the bar — crunchy and tasty like an English Toffee bar."

BAKE: 360° F. for 20 to 25 minutes

MAKES: 13x9-inch pan

Combine in mixing bowl:

¼ cup soft butter or margarine	1 teaspoon vanilla
½ cup dark corn syrup	¾ cup finely chopped nuts or coconut
⅓ cup packed brown sugar	¾ cup Hungarian® High Altitude® Flour
¼ teaspoon salt	

Mix until well blended. Spread in a greased and floured 13x9-inch pan. Bake at 360° F. for 20 to 25 minutes, or until bubbly and deep brown. Sprinkle with ½ cup **milk chocolate** or **semi-sweet chocolate chips.** Let stand 10 minutes; spread to frost. Cut into squares immediately. Chill for faster setting.

TOFFEE ALMOND CRUNCH

"Reminds you of candy — just like the name says."

BAKE: 360° F. for 20 to 25 minutes

MAKES: 13x9-inch pan

1 cup butter or margarine, melted	1 cup (6 oz.) milk chocolate or semi-sweet chocolate chips
1 cup packed brown sugar	½ cup sliced or slivered almonds
½ teaspoon instant coffee	
¼ teaspoon salt	
2 cups Hungarian® High Altitude® Flour	

Combine first 5 ingredients; blend thoroughly. Spread in bottom of ungreased 13x9-inch pan.

Bake at 360° F. for 20 to 25 minutes, or until golden brown. Sprinkle immediately with half the chocolate. Let stand 5 minutes; spread evenly. Sprinkle with half the almonds. Press almonds into chocolate with fork.

Turn out immediately onto ungreased cookie sheet. Sprinkle bottom side with remaining chocolate. Spread to frost when soft. Sprinkle with remaining almonds. When chocolate is set, break into pieces.

CHRISTMAS CONFECTIONS

"Butterscotch 'candy-like' cookies that require no baking."

MAKES: 8x8-inch pan

½ cup butter or margarine	½ cup halved candied cherries
1 cup packed brown sugar	
½ cup Hungarian® High Altitude® Flour	½ cup chopped nuts
1 egg	½ cup graham cracker crumbs

Combine in saucepan butter, brown sugar, flour, egg and cherries. Bring to boil, stirring constantly; cook 4 minutes. Stir in nuts and graham cracker crumbs. Spread in well-buttered 8x8-inch pan. Frost. Chill until firm; cut into squares.

Vanilla Icing:

Combine 1 tablespoon soft **butter**, 2 teaspoons **milk**, ½ teaspoon **vanilla** and ½ cup **powdered sugar**. Beat until smooth.

RUM SQUARES

Add 1 cup **candied fruit** and 1 teaspoon **rum** or brandy **extract**. Omit icing. Roll chilled squares in powdered sugar.

CHOCOLATE SUNDAE BARS

"A sure winner is this cookie that combines two favorite flavors — butterscotch and chocolate."

BAKE: 375° F. for 15 minutes and 15 minutes

MAKES: 9x9-inch pan

½ cup butter or margarine	½ cup salted peanuts
½ cup powdered sugar	½ cup chocolate chips
1¼ cups Hungarian® High Altitude® Flour	

Soften butter with powdered sugar. Blend in flour until particles are fine. (With mixer, use low speed.) Stir in peanuts. Press in bottom of greased 9x9, 10x8 or 11x7-inch pan. Bake at 375° F. for 15 minutes, or until light golden brown. Drizzle with Butterscotch Sauce.

Bake 15 minutes. Sprinkle immediately with chocolate chips. Let stand 10 minutes. Spread to frost.

Butterscotch Sauce:

Combine in small saucepan ¾ cup packed **brown sugar,** 2 tablespoons **butter** or margarine, and 3 tablespoons **milk.** Heat to boiling.

SKILLET FUDGE BARS

"No-bake cookies—you make them in a skillet and they taste just like the candy."

MAKES: 8x8-inch pan

¼ **cup butter or margarine**	1 **cup (6 oz.)**
1 **cup sugar**	**chocolate chips**
½ **cup Hungarian High Altitude Flour**	½ **cup chopped nuts**
	1 **teaspoon vanilla**
½ **cup half and half cream**	¼ **teaspoon salt**

Combine butter, sugar, flour and cream in skillet or saucepan. Bring to a boil, stirring constantly. Boil 5 minutes; stir occasionally. Remove from heat; stir in remaining ingredients. Pour into buttered 8x8-inch pan. Chill until firm; cut into squares.

ROCKY ROAD FUDGE

Sprinkle 1 cup **miniature marshmallows** over bottom of buttered pan. Pour **fudge** over marshmallows.

BUTTERSCOTCH FUDGE

Substitute **butterscotch pieces** for chocolate.

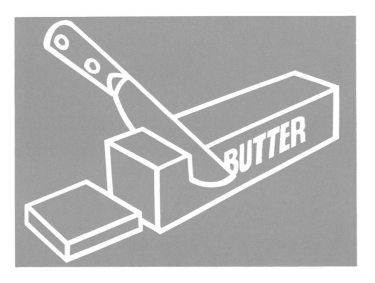

CANDY BAR COOKIES

"A butter cookie bar which you can top with any of the luscious candy toppings given below. You'll like the sweet top with the crunchy base."

BAKE: 375° F. for 15 to 20 minutes

MAKES: 9x9-inch pan

1 **cup Hungarian High Altitude Flour**	½ **cup butter or margarine**
¼ **cup powdered or granulated sugar**	¼ **teaspoon salt**

Combine ingredients in small mixing bowl. Mix on lowest speed of mixer until particles are fine or until dough forms. Press into bottom of ungreased 9x9, 10x8 or 11x7-inch pan.

Bake at 375° F. for 15 to 20 minutes, or until light golden brown. Prepare a Topping below. Spread over warm cookie base. Let set until firm. (For faster setting of Topping, place in refrigerator.) To serve, cut with sharp knife into small squares or bars.

TOPPINGS

PEANUT-DATE CREAMS

½ **cup peanut butter**	1 **cup powdered sugar**
2 **tablespoons soft butter**	2 **tablespoons milk**
1 **cup cut soft dates**	

Blend all ingredients together. Spread over baked base. Frost.

Chocolate Glaze:

Melt together ¼ cup **chocolate chips**, 1 tablespoon **butter** and 1 tablespoon **milk**. Stir in ½ cup **powdered sugar**.

CARNIVAL BARS

1 cup (6 oz.) semi-sweet chocolate pieces*	1 cup salted peanuts
¼ cup corn syrup	1½ cups colored miniature marshmallows
½ cup peanut butter	
2 tablespoons shortening	

Melt together over hot water chocolate pieces, syrup, peanut butter and shortening. Mix well. Cool slightly. Stir in peanuts and marshmallows, using as few strokes as possible. Spread over baked base.

*If you use chocolate flavored chips, omit corn syrup.

BUTTERSCOTCH CREAM BARS

½ cup corn syrup	½ cup chopped nuts or peanuts
½ cup packed brown sugar	1 cup miniature marshmallows
½ cup peanut butter	
1 cup (6 oz.) butterscotch chips	

Bring to a full boil in saucepan syrup and brown sugar. Stir in peanut butter and butterscotch pieces, then add nuts and marshmallows, using as few strokes as possible. Spread over baked base.

COCONUT MARZIPAN BARS

2 cups flaked or grated coconut	⅔ cup sweetened condensed milk
1 package (3 oz.) fruit-flavored gelatin (reserve 1 tablespoon for frosting)	

Combine all ingredients. Spoon over baked base; spread with fork. Frost.

Fruit Glaze:

Combine 1 cup **powdered sugar,** reserved gelatin, 1 tablespoon melted **butter** and 1 to 2 tablespoons **milk** until smooth and the consistency of a glaze.

MILK CHOCOLATE CANDY BARS

1 cup milk chocolate or chocolate flavored chips	½ cup chopped nuts
2 tablespoons shortening	1½ cups miniature marshmallows

Melt chocolate pieces with shortening in small saucepan over low heat. Stir in nuts and marshmallows, using as few strokes as possible. Spread over baked base.

GERMAN CREAMS

⅓ cup dairy sour cream	2 cups powdered sugar
½ cup sugar	½ cup cut candied cherries
¼ teaspoon salt	⅓ cup raisins
¼ cup butter or margarine	½ teaspoon vanilla

Boil together first 4 ingredients 5 minutes. Stir in remaining ingredients. Spread over baked base.

FILBERT CREAMS

¼ cup milk	2 cups powdered sugar
¼ cup butter or margarine	½ cup whole filberts
½ cup packed brown sugar	1 teaspoon vanilla
¼ teaspoon salt	

Boil together first 4 ingredients 5 minutes. Blend in powdered sugar until smooth. Stir in vanilla and filberts. Spread over baked base.

FRENCH CREAMS

¼ cup milk	¼ teaspoon salt
¼ cup butter or margarine	2 cups powdered sugar
½ cup sugar	½ cup almond slices
1 tablespoon cocoa	1 teaspoon vanilla
1 tablespoon instant coffee	

Boil together first 6 ingredients 5 minutes. Blend in powdered sugar until smooth. Stir in almonds and vanilla. Spread over baked base.

DATE CONFECTIONS

"No-bake caramel-like cookies with just the right amount of dates. Chocolate frosting goes on top."

MAKES: 8x8-inch pan

½ cup butter or margarine	1 egg
½ cup sugar	½ cup halved dates
½ cup packed brown sugar	½ cup chopped nuts
½ cup Hungarian® High Altitude® Flour	½ cup graham cracker crumbs

Combine in saucepan butter, sugar, brown sugar, flour, egg and dates. Bring to boil, stirring constantly; cook 4 minutes. Stir in nuts and graham cracker crumbs. Spread in well-buttered 8x8-inch pan. Frost. Chill until firm; cut into squares.

Chocolate Glaze:

Melt ¼ cup **chocolate chips** with 1 tablespoon **milk** and 1 tablespoon **butter.** Stir in ½ cup **powdered sugar;** beat until smooth.

MARSHMALLOW CRUMBLE

"For the unusual bar try this one. Melted marshmallows hold together fruit, nuts and a butter cookie."

BAKE: 375° F. for 15 to 20 minutes

MAKES: 13x9-inch pan

1½ cups Hungarian® High Altitude® Flour	1 cup raisins
½ cup sugar	1 cup halved dates
½ cup and ⅓ cup butter or margarine	1 cup pecans or walnuts
30 marshmallows or 5 cups miniature marshmallows	1 cup candied cherries or fruit

Combine flour, sugar and ½ cup butter; mix until crumbly. (With mixer, use low speed.) Place in 13x9-inch pan. Bake at 375° F. for 15 to 20 minutes, or until golden brown. Stir to break up into large pieces.

Melt marshmallows with ⅓ cup butter in saucepan over low heat; stir to blend. Meanwhile combine fruit and nuts with crumb mixture. Pour melted marshmallows over mixture. Toss to combine. Press into buttered 13x9-inch pan. Refrigerate until firm.

CEREAL "SNACK-EMS"

"A great treat and a cereal-peanut combination makes this snack inexpensive to make."

BAKE: 325° F. for 20 minutes and 30 to 35 minutes

MAKES: 13x9-inch pan

½ cup butter or margarine	2 egg whites
1½ cups bite-size shredded corn or rice cereal	1 teaspoon vanilla
	1 cup sugar
1½ cups Spanish salted peanuts	⅔ cup Hungarian® High Altitude® Flour

Combine butter, cereal and peanuts in 13x9-inch pan. Toast in 325° F. oven 20 minutes; stir once.

Beat egg whites and vanilla until foamy. Add sugar gradually, beating until stiff. Fold in flour, then the cereal-peanut mixture carefully. Spread in the 13x9-inch pan.

Bake at 325° F. for 30 to 35 minutes, or until golden brown. Loosen edges and turn out onto cookie sheet. Cool. To serve, break into pieces.

Penny Saver Idea: Use 3 cups cereal and omit peanuts. Add ½ teaspoon salt.

COCONUT TOFFEE CHEWS

"For something special in a cookie, try this toffee-like candy bar."

BAKE: 375° F. for 15 to 20 minutes

MAKES: 15x10-inch pan

½ cup butter or margarine	½ teaspoon salt
¾ cup packed brown sugar	½ teaspoon vanilla
½ cup Hungarian® High Altitude® Flour	1½ cups coconut or almond slices
¼ cup milk	1 cup (6 oz.) chocolate chips

Grease 15x10-inch pan. Line with foil; butter foil. Combine all ingredients in saucepan except chips. Heat to boiling, stirring constantly. Pour into pan.

Bake at 375° F. for 15 to 20 minutes, or until golden brown. Sprinkle with chocolate chips. Cool 5 minutes. Loosen edges. Spread chocolate chips to frost. To serve, cut with sharp knife into 1½-inch pieces.

Note: For faster setting of chocolate frosting, place pan in refrigerator a few minutes.

Tip: If you don't have a 15x10-inch pan, make one out of heavy duty foil. Place on cookie sheet.

FREEZING TIPS

Cool bars completely, then wrap for freezing. Freeze them while still fresh.

Many types of containers or wraps can be used, but always be sure it is airtight and as much air as possible has been extruded before sealing or closing.

Cut bars, pack neatly in square foil pans. Slip pan into durable polyethylene (plastic) bags. Or cut bars into large pieces and wrap for freezing.

Frostings do not freeze well, therefore, you may want to frost at the time of serving.

Freeze different kinds separately so flavors won't mingle.

For easy identification, label packages with kind and date.

Most bars thaw quickly so they can go right from the freezer to the cookie tray. If they require a longer time to thaw, leave them in the container.

FRUIT & PASTRY BARS

Pastry bars are those that are especially nice to use as little desserts. Another reason why bar cookies are so popular — they make an excellent dessert for large or small groups. An assortment of bars reminds one of a tray of French petit fours. Select several kinds for an assorted tray — rich ones, fruit ones, tea cake ones and crisp ones — and serve them as a dessert for a buffet supper. Many bars, especially those in this section, can be cut into 3-inch squares and topped with whipped cream or ice cream and served for a family dessert or at a dessert party. They are a good bring-along dessert for pot-luck dinners, church socials or picnics. Simply prepare them and carry them in the same pan. Those bars with pie-type fillings are best the day they are prepared; the fruit may make the crust soggy.

POLISH BUTTER BARS

"Butter crumb bars with a choice of fillings. Make your own, or use a can of cake and pastry filling."

BAKE: 375° F. for 25 to 30 minutes

MAKES: 9x9-inch pan

Combine in mixing bowl:

1½ cups Hungarian High Altitude® Flour	½ teaspoon salt
⅓ cup sugar	1 teaspoon vanilla
½ teaspoon baking powder	2 tablespoons milk
	½ cup butter or margarine

Mix until particles are fine, using low speed of mixer. Remove ¾ cup. Press remainder firmly into bottom of ungreased 9x9-inch pan. Spread with a Filling. Sprinkle reserved crumbs over top. Press down lightly. Bake at 375° F. for 25 to 30 minutes, or until light golden brown.

FILLINGS

KOLACKY COOKIE BARS

Combine 1 cup cut cooked **prunes** or dried **apricots, peaches** or **mixed fruit,** 1 tablespoon grated **orange peel,** ⅓ cup **sugar** and ⅛ teaspoon **nutmeg.** (Or use a 12-oz. can cake and pastry filling.)

WALNUT BARS

Combine in saucepan 1 cup **walnuts** finely chopped, grated or ground, ⅓ cup **sugar,** ¼ cup **honey,** 2 tablespoons **butter** and 1 tablespoon **milk.** Cook, stirring constantly, until hot.

DATE-NUT BARS

Combine in saucepan 1 cup haved **dates,** ½ cup finely chopped **nuts,** if desired, ¼ cup **sugar,** ¼ cup **water** and ⅛ teaspoon **mace.** Cook until thick.

POPPY SEED BARS

Combine 1¼ cups (12-oz. can) **poppy seed cake** and **pastry filling,** 2 tablespoons **honey** and ½ cup chopped **nuts.**

SWISS CHOCOLATE DESSERT BARS

"If you want to bring the 'ohs' and 'ahs' try this bar on your family and friends."

BAKE: 375° F. for 10 to 15 minutes and 25 to 30 minutes

MAKES: 13x9-inch pan

1½ cups Hungarian®High Altitude®Flour	1 cup sugar
¾ cup butter or margarine	⅛ teaspoon salt
¼ cup sugar	2 tablespoons Hungarian® High Altitude®Flour
1 bar (4 oz.) sweet cooking chocolate	2 eggs
¼ cup butter or margarine	¾ cup chopped pecans or coconut
¾ cup (small can) evaporated milk	

Mix together first 3 ingredients until particles are fine. (With mixer, use low speed.) Press into bottom of ungreased 13x9-inch pan. Bake at 375° F. for 10 to 15 minutes, or until light golden.

Melt chocolate and butter in milk over low heat. Stir until smooth. Add sugar, salt, flour and eggs; beat well. Pour over crust. Sprinkle with pecans. Bake 25 to 30 minutes.

LEMON PUFFS

"Refreshing lemon filled sponge squares are rolled in powdered sugar."

BAKE: 375° F. for 20 to 25 minutes

MAKES: 2 dozen squares

3 eggs	¾ cup Hungarian®High Altitude®Flour
⅔ cup sugar	1 can (1 lb. 4 oz.) lemon pie filling*
½ teaspoon salt	powdered sugar
1 teaspoon grated lemon peel	

Beat in small mixing bowl eggs, sugar, salt and lemon peel until thick and ivory colored. Fold in flour. Spread in 13x9-inch pan, greased and floured on bottom.

Bake at 375° F. for 20 to 25 minutes. Cool; cut in 2-inch squares. Split and fill with a teaspoonful lemon pie filling. Roll in powdered sugar.

*Or use a pie mix or your own recipe; make filling extra thick.

Tip: Cut, fill and roll puffs in powdered sugar just before serving.

SWEDISH KRINGLER BARS

"A real treat—miraculous puffy mixture tops butter pastry. Makes a great party dessert."

BAKE: 375° F. for 50 to 60 minutes

MAKES: 14x8-inch sheet

Crust:

⅓ cup butter or margarine	1 cup water
1 cup Hungarian®High Altitude®Flour	1 cup Hungarian®High Altitude®Flour
½ teaspoon salt	½ teaspoon salt
2 to 3 tablespoons water	½ teaspoon almond extract
	3 eggs
Topping:	¼ cup chopped almonds, if desired
½ cup butter or margarine	

Crust: Cut butter into flour and salt. Add water gradually while stirring with a fork just until a dough can be formed. Form into a square. Coat well with flour. Roll out on cookie sheet to 14x8-inch rectangle.

Topping: Melt butter in water. Stir in flour and salt. Cook, stirring constantly, until very thick and mixture leaves side of pan. Add almond extract and eggs, one at a time, beating well after each. Stir in almonds. Spread over pie crust.

Bake at 375° F. for 50 to 60 minutes, or until rich golden brown. Frost warm.

Almond Icing:

Combine 1 cup **powdered sugar,** 2 tablespoons soft **butter** or margarine, 1 tablespoon **milk** and ½ teaspoon **almond extract.** Beat until smooth.

LEMON CREAM CHEESERS

"Lemon flavored cheese cake in a bar cookie. Ideal dessert for buffet supper."

BAKE: 375° F. for 30 to 40 minutes

MAKES: 8 or 9-inch square pan

½ cup butter or margarine	⅓ cup sugar
1¼ cups Hungarian High Altitude Flour	1 egg
½ cup quick-cooking rolled oats	2 teaspoons grated lemon peel
½ cup packed brown sugar	1 tablespoon lemon juice
¼ teaspoon salt	¼ cup milk
1 package (8 oz.) soft cream cheese	

Combine first 5 ingredients; mix until particles are fine. (With mixer, use low speed.) Press half of mixture into bottom of ungreased 8 or 9-inch square pan.

Combine remaining ingredients; beat until smooth and creamy. Pour over crust. Top with remaining crumb mixture. Bake at 375° F. for 30 to 40 minutes. Store cooled bars in refrigerator.

LEMON FILLERS

"Luscious lemon pie filling baked between a butter crust. Perfect mini-dessert for a coffee party."

BAKE: 375° F. for 15 minutes and 25 to 30 minutes

MAKES: 13x9-inch pan

½ cup butter or margarine	2 cups Hungarian High Altitude Flour
¼ cup shortening	¼ teaspoon salt
½ cup sugar	

Mix together all ingredients until particles are fine. (With mixer, use low speed.) Remove 1 cup. Press remainder into bottom of ungreased 13x9-inch pan. Bake at 375° F. for 15 minutes. Spread Filling over partially baked crust. Sprinkle with reserved crumbs. If desired, drizzle with Glaze. Bake 25 to 30 minutes, or until golden brown.

Lemon Filling:

1 cup sugar	1 tablespoon grated lemon peel
3 tablespoons Hungarian High Altitude Flour	¼ cup lemon juice
2 slightly beaten eggs	2 tablespoons butter
¾ cup water	

Combine sugar and flour in saucepan. Stir in remaining ingredients. Cook over medium high heat, stirring constantly, until very thick.

Glaze:

Combine ½ cup **powdered sugar** and 1 tablespoon **cream** or milk.

CHERRY STREUSEL BARS

"Easy to make, yet so special are these colorful cherry bars with their streusel topping."

BAKE: 375° F. for 12 to 15 minutes and 25 to 30 minutes

MAKES: 13x9-inch pan

⅔ cup butter or margarine	1 can (1 lb. 4 oz.) cherry pie filling
2 cups Hungarian High Altitude Flour	½ cup coconut or chopped nuts, if desired
½ cup sugar	

Cut butter into flour and sugar until particles are fine. (With mixer, use low speed.) Set aside 1 cup. Press remainder into bottom of greased 13x9-inch pan. Bake at 375° F. for 12 to 15 minutes, or until golden brown.

Spoon cherries over partially baked crust. Combine coconut with reserved flour-sugar mixture. Sprinkle over cherries. Bake 25 to 30 minutes, or until light golden brown.

CHERRY PASTRY PETITES

"A perfect little dessert to have after a dinner party — delicious yet easy to take to a special event."

BAKE: 375° F. for 15 minutes and 25 to 30 minutes

MAKES: 13x9-inch pan

2 cups Hungarian® High Altitude® Flour	⅓ cup sugar
¾ cup butter or margarine	1 egg
¾ cup sugar	¼ cup cut maraschino cherries
½ teaspoon salt	¼ cup almond slices
1 package (8 oz.) cream cheese	½ cup chocolate chips

Combine first 4 ingredients. Beat on low speed of mixer until particles are fine. Press ⅔ of mixture firmly into bottom of ungreased 13x9-inch pan. Bake at 375° F. for 15 minutes.

Blend together cream cheese, sugar and egg until smooth and creamy. Stir in remaining ingredients. Spread over partially baked crust. Sprinkle with remaining crumbs.

Bake 25 to 30 minutes, or until light golden brown.

PECAN PIE BARS

"Just like little pieces of pie and just the right size for this rich dessert."

BAKE: 375° F. for 15 minutes and 25 to 30 minutes

MAKES: 9x9-inch pan

1 cup and 1 tablespoon Hungarian® High Altitude® Flour	3 eggs
½ cup rolled oats	¾ cup light or dark corn syrup
¾ cup packed brown sugar	1 cup broken pecans
½ cup butter or margarine	1 teaspoon vanilla
	¼ teaspoon salt

Mix together 1 cup flour, oats, ¼ cup brown sugar and butter until particles are fine. (With mixer, use low speed.) Press into bottom of greased 9x9-inch pan.

Bake at 375° F. for 15 minutes, or until light golden. Beat together eggs, syrup, pecans, vanilla, salt, ½ cup brown sugar and 1 tablespoon flour. Pour over partially baked crust. Bake 25 to 30 minutes.

SOUTHERN COCONUT BARS
Substitute 1 cup **coconut** for the pecans.

APPLE QUICK PIE BARS

"Apple pie and apple quick are combined in a bar which is topped with a tart lemon glaze."

BAKE: 375° F. for 15 minutes and 30 to 35 minutes

MAKES: 13x9-inch pan

½ cup shortening	3 to 4 tablespoons milk
¼ cup and 2 tablespoons butter or margarine	4 cups chopped, pared apples
2 cups Hungarian® High Altitude® Flour	½ cup quick-cooking rolled oats
1 teaspoon salt	½ cup brown sugar

Cut shortening and ¼ cup butter into flour and salt until fine. Set aside 1 cup. To remainder add milk gradually while stirring lightly with fork until dough is moist enough to hold together. Form into a square. Flatten slightly; smooth edges. Roll out on floured surface to 13x9-inch rectangle. Place in bottom of ungreased 13x9-inch pan.

Bake at 375° F. for 15 minutes. Top with apples. Combine oats, brown sugar and 2 tablespoons butter with reserved crumbs. Sprinkle over apples. Bake 30 to 35 minutes, or until apples are tender. (If top becomes too dark before apples are tender, cover with foil.) If desired, drizzle with Glaze while warm.

Lemon Glaze:

Combine 1 tablespoon **butter** or margarine, 2 tablespoons **lemon juice** and ½ cup **powdered sugar**.

QUICK AS-A-MIX FAVORITES

The one-step method of baking developed in the Hungarian High Altitude Kitchens is so easy that homemakers told us the recipes were as quick-as-a mix to make. All the recipes in this section are made by that easy method — place all ingredients in mixing bowl and beat 1 or 2 minutes. Many of these favorites are like little teacakes and make an excellent snack for a late evening party when something a little sweet but not too rich is desired. They are ideal for a coffee party or kids will love them with a glass of milk or as a special treat in their lunch box. Throughout this book you'll find bar cookie recipes that you can mix up and have ready for the oven in 5 minutes or less.

LEMON CAKE BARS

"Little pieces of cake-like bars always add a refreshing touch to the end of the meal."

BAKE: 360° F. for 30 to 35 minutes

MAKES: 15x10-inch pan

Combine in mixing bowl:

2 cups Hungarian® High Altitude® Flour	⅓ cup shortening
1¼ cups sugar	¼ cup soft butter or margarine
1 package (3¾ oz.) instant lemon pudding mix	½ cup currants, if desired
1 teaspoon salt	3 eggs
1½ teaspoons baking powder	1 cup milk

Blend, then beat at medium speed 2 minutes. Turn into 15x10x1-inch pan, greased and floured on the bottom.

Bake at 360° F. for 30 to 35 minutes, or until top springs back when touched lightly in center. Frost warm. Sprinkle with **powdered sugar** before serving.

Note: Bars may be baked in two 9x9-inch pans.

Lemon 'n Orange Glaze:

Combine 1 cup **powdered sugar**, 2 tablespoons **orange juice**, 1 tablespoon **lemon juice** and 2 tablespoons melted **butter** or margarine.

44

BANANA SLIMS

"Moist bars that can be used as bar cookies or substitute for cake or any dessert. The Streusel bars are good topped with whipped or ice cream."

BAKE: 375° F. for 20 to 25 minutes

MAKES: 15x10-inch pan

Combine in mixing bowl:

1½ cups Hungarian® High Altitude® Flour	2 eggs
1 cup granulated or brown sugar	1 medium very ripe banana, sliced
½ teaspoon soda	⅓ cup milk
½ teaspoon salt	1 teaspoon lemon juice
½ cup shortening	½ cup chopped nuts
	½ teaspoon baking powder

Blend, then beat at medium speed 2 minutes. Spread in greased 15x10-inch pan.

Bake at 375° F. for 20 to 25 minutes, or until top springs back when touched lightly in center. Cool and frost with Banana, Butterscotch or Browned Butter Frosting. (See Frosting Section.)

BANANA CAKE BARS:

Bake in a greased 13x9-inch pan. Bake 25 to 30 minutes.

BANANA STREUSEL BARS:

Combine ½ cup **sugar**, ⅓ cup **Hungarian® High Altitude® Flour**, ¼ teaspoon **nutmeg** and 3 tablespoons **butter** or **margarine** until particles are fine. Sprinkle over batter in pan. Baked bars need no frosting.

TWO TONE BROWNIES

"Tremendous to eat—a layer of butterscotch and chocolate brownies all made by 'quick-as-a-mix method.'"

BAKE: 350° F. for 30 to 40 minutes

MAKES: 9x9-inch pan

Combine in mixing bowl:

¾ cup Hungarian® High Altitude® Flour	1 teaspoon vanilla
1 cup packed brown sugar	½ teaspoon salt
½ cup shortening	½ cup chopped nuts
2 eggs	

Blend, then beat at medium speed until well blended, about 1 minute. Spread half of batter in greased 9x9, 11x7 or 10x8-inch pan.

To remaining batter, blend in 1 ounce no-melt **unsweetened chocolate.** Spread carefully over light batter.

Bake at 350° F. for 30 to 40 minutes. Frost, if desired, with Chocolate Icing. (See Frosting Section.)

YOUNG COOKS

Because bar cookies are so easy and foolproof to make and bake, they are good recipes for the beginner to use. Some recipes the young cook will want to try are: Fudge Brownies, Peanut Butter Strips, Peanut Butter Squares, Chocolate Chip Bars, Chewy Oatmeal Bars, Gumdrop Bars, Gingersnap Chews, Blonde Brownies.

DATE NUT CREAMS

"Browned butter frosting completes this sour cream date bar — it's a perfect blend of flavors."

BAKE: 375° F. for 20 to 25 minutes

MAKES: 15x10-inch pan

Combine in mixing bowl:

1⅔ cups Hungarian® High Altitude® Flour	½ teaspoon soda
⅓ cup shortening	1 teaspoon salt
1 cup packed brown sugar	1 teaspoon vanilla
2 eggs	1 cup dates, cut in pieces
1 cup dairy sour cream	½ cup chopped nuts, if desired
¼ cup water	
½ teaspoon baking powder	

Blend, then beat at medium speed 1 minute. Spread in greased 15x10-inch pan.

Bake at 375° F. for 20 to 25 minutes, or until light golden brown. Frost warm with Browned Butter Frosting. (See Frosting Section.)

TOASTY PECAN SQUARES

"Butter cake bars with toasty pecans in the bar and frosting."

BAKE: 375° F. for 20 to 25 minutes

MAKES: 13x9-inch pan

Brown together in skillet:

¼ cup butter	½ teaspoon salt
¾ cup finely chopped pecans	1 teaspoon vanilla
	⅓ cup shortening

Combine in mixing bowl:

1½ cups Hungarian® High Altitude® Flour	2 eggs
1 cup sugar	⅔ cup milk
1½ teaspoons baking powder	½ cup toasted pecan mixture

Blend, then beat at medium speed 2 minutes. Turn into 13x9-inch pan, greased and floured on the bottom.

Bake at 375° F. for 20 to 25 minutes, or until top springs back when touched lightly. Cool and frost.

Pecan Frosting:

Beat together 2 tablespoons **milk,** 2 cups **powdered sugar** and remaining pecan-butter mixture. Add a few drops **milk** if needed.

Note: For a thinner bar, bake in a 15x10-inch pan for 15 to 20 minutes.

ORANGE PECAN BARS

*"Sour cream is the secret of this moist,
rich orange bar."*
BAKE: 375° F. for 25 to 30 minutes
MAKES: 13x9-inch pan

Combine in mixing bowl:

1½ cups Hungarian® High Altitude® Flour	2 eggs
½ cup soft butter or margarine	½ cup dairy sour cream
½ cup packed brown sugar	½ teaspoon soda
½ teaspoon baking powder	½ teaspoon salt
¼ cup sugar	1 tablespoon grated orange peel
	½ cup chopped pecans

Blend, then beat at medium speed 2 minutes. Spread in greased 13x9-inch pan. Bake at 375° F. for 25 to 30 minutes, or until top springs back when touched lightly in center. Frost warm with Orange Frosting. (See Frosting Section.)

LEMON NUT CREAMS

*"Lemon in the bar and in the frosting makes
these bars extra refreshing."*
BAKE: 375° F. for 20 to 25 minutes
MAKES: 13x9-inch pan

Combine in mixing bowl:

1⅓ cups Hungarian® High Altitude® Flour	⅓ cup soft butter or margarine
1 cup sugar	2 eggs
½ teaspoon baking powder	1 tablespoon grated lemon peel
½ teaspoon salt	½ cup chopped nuts
⅓ cup milk	

Blend, then beat at medium speed 2 minutes. Spread in greased and floured 13x9-inch pan.

Bake at 375° F. for 20 to 25 minutes, or until top springs back when touched lightly in center. Frost immediately with Lemon Frosting. (See Frosting Section.)

GOLDEN NUGGETS

*"Delicious and nutritious are these delicately light
bars. The popular carrot cake now made as a bar."*
BAKE: 375° F. for 25 to 30 minutes
MAKES: 13x9-inch pan

Combine in mixing bowl:

1 cup plus 2 tablespoons Hungarian High Altitude® Flour	½ teaspoon soda
1 cup sugar	1 teaspoon salt
2 eggs	1 teaspoon cinnamon
½ cup cooking oil	½ cup chopped nuts
1½ cups finely shredded carrots	¼ cup milk
	½ teaspoon baking powder

Blend, then beat at medium speed 2 minutes. Pour into greased 13x9-inch pan.

Bake at 375° F. for 25 to 30 minutes, or until top springs back when touched lightly. Frost warm with Sour Cream Frosting. (See Frosting Section.)

A COOKIE TRAY
Include a variety of textures and flavors. Also cut bars into small pieces so each person can sample more than one kind. Four or five kinds is a nice variety. Here's a nice selection — Coco-Roons Chocolate-in-Oatmeal Bars, Ginger Cream Bars, Swedish Tea Cakes and Austrian Butter Cookies.

CHOCOLATE CHIP SOFTIES

"Soft chocolate chip sour cream cookies taste extra good with a browned butter frosting."

BAKE: 375° F. for 25 to 35 minutes

MAKES: 15x10-inch pan

Combine in mixing bowl:

2 cups Hungarian High Altitude® Flour	1 teaspoon vanilla
½ cup soft butter or margarine	½ teaspoon soda
1 cup packed brown sugar	½ teaspoon salt
2 eggs	1 cup (6 oz.) chocolate chips
1 cup dairy sour cream	½ cup chopped nuts

Blend, then beat at low speed 2 minutes. Spread in greased 15x10-inch pan.

Bake at 375° F. for 25 to 35 minutes, or until top springs back when touched lightly. Frost warm with Browned Butter Frosting. (See Frosting Section.)

GINGER CREAM BARS

"Quick-as-a-mix, soft, moist, spicy bars complemented with an orange frosting."

BAKE: 350° F. for 25 to 30 minutes

MAKES: 15x10-inch pan

Combine in mixing bowl:

2 cups Hungarian® High Altitude® Flour	½ teaspoon cinnamon
⅔ cup sugar	¼ teaspoon cloves
¾ teaspoon soda	½ cup shortening
½ teaspoon salt	½ cup light molasses
½ teaspoon nutmeg	½ cup boiling water
	1 egg

Blend, then beat at medium speed 2 minutes. Spread in greased 15x10-inch pan.

Bake at 350° F. for 25 to 30 minutes, or until top springs back when touched lightly in center. Frost warm with Orange Frosting. (See Frosting Section.)

SUGAR 'N SPICE TEACAKES

"A touch of Sweden — spicy and warm and ready to eat hot from the oven."

Prepare batter for Ginger Cream Bars; spread in pan. Sprinkle batter with a mixture of 3 tablespoons **sugar**, ⅓ cup **almond slices** and 1 tablespoon grated **orange peel.**

LEMON 'N CHEESE TOPPING

Soften 3 ounces **cream cheese** with 1 tablespoon **lemon peel,** 1 teaspoon **lemon juice** and ¼ cup **sugar.** Gradually add ½ cup **whipping cream,** beating until thick. Serve on squares of Sugar 'n Spice Teacakes.

SPICY PUMPKIN BARS

"Pumpkin pie flavor in a moist bar. Try it with whipped or ice cream for dessert."

BAKE: 375° F. for 25 to 30 minutes

MAKES: 13x9-inch pan

Combine in mixing bowl:

1 cup plus 2 tablespoons Hungarian®High Altitude® Flour	¼ cup milk
	1 teaspoon vanilla
1 cup granulated or brown sugar	¼ teaspoon soda
	½ teaspoon salt
⅓ cup cooking oil or soft shortening	2 eggs
	¼ cup chopped nuts, if desired
1 cup canned pumpkin	
1 teaspoon baking powder	
2 teaspoons pumpkin pie spice*	

Blend, then beat at medium speed 2 minutes. Spread in 13x9-inch pan, greased and floured on bottom.

Bake at 375° F. for 25 to 30 minutes, or until top springs back when touched lightly. Frost with Browned Butter or Sour Cream Frosting, or Penuche Broiled Topping. (See Frosting Section.)

*One teaspoon cinnamon, ½ teaspoon ginger and ¼ teaspoon nutmeg may be substituted for pumpkin pie spice.

BLACK WALNUT QUICKIES

"For those who like real chewy moist bars — caramel-like sauce completes a black walnut bar. Use other nuts if you prefer."

BAKE: 350° F. for 20 to 25 minutes

MAKES: 9x9-inch pan

Combine in mixing bowl:

1 cup Hungarian®High Altitude® Flour	¼ teaspoon baking powder
½ cup sugar	2 eggs
½ cup packed brown sugar	½ cup chopped black walnuts
½ teaspoon salt	

Blend, then beat at medium speed 1 minute. Spread in greased 9x9, 10x8 or 11x7-inch pan.

Bake at 350° F. for 20 to 25 minutes. Spread with Topping. Broil 2 to 5 minutes, or until bubbly and golden brown.

Brown Sugar Topping:

Combine ⅓ cup **brown sugar**, 2 tablespoons soft **butter** and 2 tablespoons **milk.**

49

ALL TIME FAVORITES

Like apple pie, bar cookies are an all-American favorite. All of those old and all-time favorites can be found in this section. To make it easy for today's busy homemaker we've updated and streamlined the method for making the bars and retained all of that homemade goodness. You're also going to like some of the new twists to Brownies and other old favorites. One of the best desserts you can serve is brownies topped with ice cream and chocolate sauce.

BLONDE BROWNIES

"Lunch Box Treat—chewy bars are full of chocolate pieces and nuts."

BAKE: 375° F. for 25 to 30 minutes

MAKES: 13x9-inch pan

½ cup butter or margarine	¼ teaspoon baking powder
1⅓ cups packed brown sugar	½ teaspoon salt
2 eggs	½ cup chopped nuts
1½ cups Hungarian® High Altitude® Flour	½ cup chocolate chips, if desired
1 teaspoon vanilla	

Melt butter in 2-quart saucepan. Stir in remaining ingredients except chocolate chips. Spread in greased and floured 13x9-inch pan. Sprinkle with chocolate chips.

Bake at 375° F. for 25 to 30 minutes. Serve plain, sprinkled with powdered sugar or frosted with Browned Butter Icing. (See Frosting Section.)

COBBLESTONE BLONDE BROWNIES

Prepare Blonde Brownies omitting nuts and chips. After spreading dough in pan, sprinkle with ½ cup chopped **nuts** or **chocolate chips** and 1 cup **miniature marshmallows.**

SWEDISH BLONDE BROWNIES

Prepare Blonde Brownies omitting nuts and chips. Bake 25 minutes. Meanwhile prepare **Tosca Topping:** Combine in small saucepan ½ cup **sugar,** ¼ cup **butter,** 2 tablespoons **Hungarian® High Altitude® Flour** and 2 tablespoons **cream.** Boil 2 minutes. Stir in ¾ cup **almond slices** and ¼ teaspoon **almond extract.** Spread over hot baked bars. Bake 5 minutes or until hot and bubbly all over.

FUDGE BROWNIES

"Chewy and rich are these moist brownies—plus easy to make."

BAKE: 350° F. for 25 to 30 minutes

MAKES: 9x9-inch pan*

2 ounces or packets unsweetened chocolate	⅔ cup Hungarian® High Altitude® Flour
½ cup butter or margarine	¼ teaspoon baking powder
1 cup granulated or packed brown sugar	½ teaspoon vanilla
2 eggs	¼ teaspoon salt
	½ cup finely chopped nuts, if desired

Melt chocolate with butter and sugar in 2-quart saucepan. Remove from heat; stir in remaining ingredients. Spread in greased 9x9, 10x8 or 11x7-inch pan. Bake at 350° F. for 25 to 30 minutes. Cool and frost with Chocolate Frosting. (See Frosting Section.) If desired, sprinkle with chopped nuts.

*A 10x8, 11x7 or 8x8-inch pan may be used. In the 8x8-inch pan the brownies are thick and extra moist; bake 30 to 40 minutes.

Tip: Vary the chocolate level to suit your family's taste. If you like less chocolate, use 1½ ounces or go to 1 ounce for a milk chocolate flavor.

ROCKY ROAD BROWNIES

Sprinkle hot baked Brownies immediately with 1 cup **miniature marshmallows.** Drizzle frosting over all.

PEANUT BUTTER BROWNIES

Add ¼ cup **peanut butter** to batter for Fudge Brownies. Add 2 tablespoons **peanut butter** to frosting.

'MALLOW BROWNIES

Top hot baked brownies with **marshmallow halves,** cut-side down. Place close together (18 whole marshmallows for 8x8-inch pan and 21 for 9x9-inch pan.) Place in oven 3 minutes. Frost warm. Sprinkle with **coconut,** if desired. Easier to cut if allowed to stand several hours.

LAZY DAISY BROWNIES

Do not frost. Top baked brownies with a mixture of 2 tablespoons soft **butter,** 1 tablespoon **milk,** ½ cup **brown sugar** and ½ cup **coconut.** Broil until hot and bubbly, 2 to 5 minutes.

CHRISTMAS BROWNIES

Add ½ cup of each to Fudge Brownie batter — **raisins,** cut **dates,** and cut **candied cherries.**

COCONUT BROWNIES

Omit nuts and add 2 cups (7 oz.) cookie or grated **coconut** to Fudge Brownie batter. (Especially good with only 1 ounce of chocolate in Brownie batter.)

CHERRY BROWNIES

Add ½ cup cut **maraschino cherries** to batter for Fudge Brownies. Add 2 tablespoons cut **cherries** to frosting.

SUPER DESSERT IDEAS

Bake **Fudge Brownies** or any of the variations in a greased 9 or 10-inch piepan at 325° F. To serve, cut into small wedges. For a'la mode brownies, top the unfrosted brownies with ice cream, then drizzle with chocolate sauce and sprinkle with salted nuts. Cut into wedges.

DREAM BARS

"This old favorite is a must on a cookie tray."

BAKE: 375° F. for 15 minutes and 20 to 25 minutes

MAKES: 9x9-inch pan

1 cup Hungarian® High Altitude® Flour	1 teaspoon vanilla
1⅓ cups packed brown sugar	¼ teaspoon baking powder
⅓ cup soft butter or margarine	¼ teaspoon salt
2 eggs	1 cup flaked coconut
	½ cup chopped nuts, if desired

Mix together flour, ⅓ cup brown sugar and butter until particles are fine. (With mixer, use low speed.) Press into bottom of ungreased 9x9, 10x8 or 11x7-inch pan. Bake at 375° F. for 15 minutes, or until light brown.

Combine 1 cup brown sugar and remaining ingredients in mixing bowl. Beat at medium speed until thick and foamy. Pour over partially baked crust. Bake at 375° F. for 20 to 25 minutes, or until golden brown.

ORANGE OR LEMON DREAM BARS

Add 1 tablespoon grated **orange or lemon peel** to the egg mixture. Frost warm bars with the Orange or Lemon Frosting, (See Frosting Section.) (It will take only half the recipe.)

DREAM BAR CHIPS

Dream Bars are sure to please the youngsters if you substitute ½ cup **chocolate chips** for the coconut or nuts.

MATRIMONIAL (DATE) BARS

"A date filling baked between layers of crunchy oatmeal cookie. Try one of the other fruit fillings."

BAKE: 350° F. for 30 to 35 minutes

MAKES: 13x9-inch pan

Date Filling:	Cookie Base:
1¼ cups (8 oz.) halved dates	¾ cup butter or margarine
½ cup water	1 cup packed brown sugar
¼ cup sugar	½ teaspoon salt
1 tablespoon lemon juice	1½ cups Hungarian® High Altitude® Flour
	1 cup rolled oats

Combine Filling ingredients in saucepan. Cook over medium heat, stirring occasionally, until thick and smooth.

Cream butter with brown sugar and salt. Blend in flour and oats until particles are fine. Press ⅔ of crumb mixture into bottom of greased 13x9-inch pan. Spread with filling. Sprinkle with remaining crumbs; press down lightly.

Bake at 350° F. for 30 to 35 minutes, or until golden brown.

RAISIN BARS

Combine in saucepan 1½ cups ground or chopped **raisins**, 2 tablespoons grated **orange peel**, ¼ cup **orange juice**, ⅓ cup **water** and ¼ cup **sugar**. Cook until thick.

APRICOT BARS

Cook 1⅓ cups cut dried **apricots**, ½ cup **water** and 1 tablespoon **lemon juice** until apricots are tender. Stir in ½ cup **sugar**; cook until thick.

MINCEMEATERS' SANDWICH BARS

Use 2 cups prepared **mincemeat** for filling.

DATE NUT SQUARES

*"Chewy with dates and crunchy with nuts.
Makes an easy family dessert.
Serve warm with whipped cream."*

BAKE: 325° F. for 50 to 60 minutes

MAKES: 36

Combine in mixing bowl:

¾ cup Hungarian® High Altitude® Flour	½ teaspoon salt
½ cup plus ⅓ cup packed brown sugar	2 eggs
1 teaspoon baking powder	2 tablespoons cooking oil
1 teaspoon vanilla	1 cup dates, cut in pieces
	½ cup chopped nuts

Beat at low speed 2 minutes. Spread in greased and floured 9x9, 10x8 or 11x7-inch pan.

Bake at 325° F. for 50 to 60 minutes. Cool. Cut into 1½-inch squares. Coat with **powdered sugar.**

OLD-FASHIONED SUGAR COOKIES

*"Crisp sugar cookies made the easy way.
Baked cookies may be frosted."*

BAKE: 360° F. for 12 to 15 minutes

MAKES: 5 to 6 dozen

2 cups Hungarian® High Altitude® Flour	½ teaspoon salt
⅔ cup sugar	¾ cup butter or margarine
1 teaspoon vanilla	2 tablespoons milk
	1 egg

Place ingredients in mixing bowl. Mix on low speed of mixer until dough forms. Divide in half. Form into square. Roll out each half on greased cookie sheet with floured rolling pin or press with floured fingers to 14x10-inch rectangle; smooth edges. Sprinkle with plain or colored **sugar.**

Bake at 360° F. for 12 to 15 minutes, or ur golden brown. Immediately cut 2-inch squar monds or triangles and remove from cookie s

Tip: If cookie sheet slips while rolling out d place on damp paper toweling or cloth. If edges brown faster, cut into squares and remove the outside squares. Brown remaining cookies to desired brownness.

CHRISTMAS FRUIT CONFECTION

"A European fruitcake bar — rich with candied fruit and rolled in powdered sugar before serving."

BAKE: 325° F. for 50 to 60 minutes.

MAKES: 8 or 9-inch square pan

¾ cup sugar	1 cup coarsely chopped almonds or other nuts
⅓ cup honey	1 teaspoon rum or brandy extract
¼ cup water	
¼ cup butter or margarine	¼ teaspoon baking powder
¾ cup Hungarian® High Altitude® Flour	½ teaspoon salt
1 egg	
1 cup raisins	
1½ cups mixed candied fruit (half candied cherries)	

Line 8 or 9-inch square pan with foil. Grease foil. Boil together sugar, honey, water and butter for 3 minutes. Remove from heat. Stir in remaining ingredients. Pour into prepared pan.

Bake at 325° F. for 50 to 60 minutes. Cool. Cut into squares; coat with **powdered sugar.** (For rum balls, shape baked squares into balls and roll in powdered sugar.)

PRALINE CANDY BARS

"Cookies that are chewy and rich with brown sugar and nuts, and topped with a praline frosting."

BAKE: 350° F. for 25 to 30 minutes

MAKES: 13x9-inch pan

Combine in mixing bowl:

1⅔ cups Hungarian® High Altitude® Flour	2 tablespoons milk
1¼ cups packed brown sugar	¾ teaspoon baking powder
1 egg	1 teaspoon vanilla
½ cup soft butter or margarine	¼ teaspoon salt
	½ cup broken pecans

Beat at low speed 2 minutes. Spread in greased 13x9-inch pan. Sprinkle with ½ cup broken **pecans.**

Bake at 350° F. for 25 to 30 minutes, or until light golden brown. Cool. Drizzle with Frosting.

Praline Frosting:
Melt together ½ cup packed **brown sugar,** 2 tablespoons **butter** and 1 tablespoon **milk.** Stir in ½ cup **powdered sugar.**

GUMDROP BARS

"Chewy, moist brown sugar bars that are full of gumdrops."

BAKE: 375° F. for 25 to 30 minutes

MAKES: 13x9-inch pan

½ cup butter or margarine	1 teaspoon vanilla
1⅓ cups packed brown sugar	¼ teaspoon baking powder
2 eggs	½ teaspoon salt
1½ cups Hungarian® High Altitude® Flour	½ cup chopped nuts
	1 cup cut gumdrops

Melt butter in saucepan. Stir in remaining ingredients. Spread in greased and floured 13x9-inch pan.

Bake at 375° F. for 25 to 30 minutes, or until golden brown. Sprinkle with powdered sugar, or frost with Butterscotch or Orange Frosting. (See Frosting Section.) Cool completely; cut into bars.

SUGAR 'N CHIP BARS

Your kids will say—"Chocolate chip cookies have never been this good."

BAKE: 360° F. for 25 to 30 minutes

MAKES: 15x10-inch pan

1 cup butter or margarine	1 cup (6 oz.) chocolate chips
1 cup sugar	½ cup chopped nuts, if desired
¾ teaspoon baking powder	2 cups Hungarian® High Altitude® Flour
1 teaspoon vanilla	
½ teaspoon salt	

Cream together butter, sugar, baking powder, vanilla and salt. Blend in remaining ingredients. Press or spread into bottom of an ungreased 15x10-inch pan.

Bake at 360° F. for 25 to 30 minutes, or until light golden brown. Cut into squares while warm.

Tip: For a thicker bar, bake in a 13x9-inch pan for 30 to 35 minutes.

PEANUT MERINGUE BARS

"Brown sugar bars are topped with a brown sugar meringue full of salted peanuts."

BAKE: 325° F. for 15 minutes and 35 minutes

MAKES: 13x9-inch pan

1½ cups Hungarian® High Altitude® Flour	2 eggs, separated
1½ cups packed brown sugar	1 teaspoon vanilla
	¼ teaspoon salt
⅓ cup shortening	½ cup chocolate chips
¼ cup butter or margarine	½ cup salted peanuts

Mix together flour, ½ cup brown sugar, shortening, butter and egg yolks until particles are fine. (With mixer, use low speed.) Press into bottom of ungreased 13x9-inch pan. Bake at 325° F. for 15 to 20 minutes, or until light golden.

Beat egg whites with vanilla and salt until foamy. Gradually add 1 cup brown sugar; continue beating until very stiff peaks form when beaters are raised. Fold in chocolate chips and peanuts. Spread carefully over partially baked crust.

Bake 35 minutes. Cut into bars with wet, sharp knife.

CHOCOLATE TEA CAKES

"Rich chocolate squares make a delightful addition to any cookie tray."

BAKE: 350° F. for 25 to 30 minutes

MAKES: 72

1 cup butter or margarine	2 cups Hungarian® High Altitude® Flour
1 package (4 oz.) chocolate pudding and pie filling mix	½ cup chopped nuts
¼ cup sugar	½ cup powdered sugar
	1 tablespoon cocoa

Cream butter with pudding mix and sugar. Blend in flour and nuts. Press into ungreased 13x9-inch pan. Bake at 350° F. for 25 to 30 minutes. Cool 10 minutes. Cut into 1¼-inch squares, roll in mixture of powdered sugar and cocoa.

PREPARE TO BAKE

Before you start to mix a recipe, read the recipe. Be sure you have all the necessary ingredients. Also preheat the oven. All the baking times are determined after the oven has reached the designated temperature. For more specific help in baking, read **The Mixing and Baking Terms** on page 31, the section **Know Your Ingredients** at the beginning of the book and **Baking Aids,** page 22.

COOKIE FROSTINGS

For many bar cookies a thin layer of frosting enhances the flavor of the bar. Sometimes so thin, we call it a glaze. If bars are frosted cold, the frosting should be of a consistency that holds a shallow swirl and has a soft look. When bars are frosted warm, the frosting will melt and some of the flavor will go right into the baked product. Start with a thicker product than when frosting bars that have cooled completely.

Frostings tend to thicken, especially those starting with a hot mixture or liquid, as they stand; thin with a few drops of milk or cream.

If the powdered (confectioners') sugar is lumpy, press through a sieve or strainer. Or expect to beat longer and harder to make it smooth.

To measure powdered sugar, spoon it lightly into the cup, then level off across the top with a metal spatula.

A sprinkle of nuts or coconut can be used to decorate the frosting.

A few drops of food coloring adds a party look to a Vanilla Frosting.

Frostings generally do not freeze well. They tend to dry out or get what is sometimes called a freezer burn. It is recommended to freeze bars unfrosted, then frost at time of serving. Even if the bar is frosted warm, do not frost. At time of frosting use a thinner frosting.

For Browned Butter Frosting, use butter; margarine will not brown. The margarine can be melted and used, but you will not have a brown butter flavor or color.

If you stack frosted bars or cookies in a container be sure the frosting has set. It is a good idea to lay waxed paper between the layers.

If you use skim milk in frosting, start out with about ½ less than the amount of milk called for in the recipe.

An easy chocolate frosting is to sprinkle hot bars with chocolate chips; let stand a few minutes (do not place in oven) and spread to frost. If desired, place a few small spoonfuls of peanut butter on the bars too and spread with the chocolate.

ORANGE OR LEMON FROSTING

2 cups powdered sugar
2 tablespoons soft butter or margarine
1 tablespoon grated orange or lemon peel
2 tablespoons orange or lemon juice

Combine all ingredients. Beat until smooth and creamy, adding more orange juice if necessary. Frosts 13x9 or 15x10-inch pan.

BANANA FROSTING

2 tablespoons soft butter or margarine
2 cups powdered sugar
¼ teaspoon salt
½ medium ripe banana

Combine all ingredients. Beat until smooth and creamy, adding few drops **milk,** if necessary. Frosts 13x9 or 15x10-inch pan.

CHOCOLATE FROSTING

2 ounces unsweetened chocolate
¼ cup butter or margarine
2 tablespoons milk
2 cups powdered sugar

Melt together chocolate, butter and milk. Stir in powdered sugar, adding more milk, if necessary. Frosts 13x9 or 15x10-inch pan.

CHOCOLATE ICING

1 ounce unsweetened chocolate
2 tablespoons butter or margarine
1 tablespoon milk
1 cup powdered sugar

Melt together chocolate, butter and milk. Stir in powdered sugar, adding more milk, if necessary. Frosts 9x9, 10x8, 11x7, 8x8-inch pan.

BUTTERSCOTCH FROSTING

2 tablespoons butter or margarine
¼ cup packed brown sugar
2 tablespoons milk or cream
2 cups powdered sugar
½ teaspoon vanilla

Melt together butter, brown sugar and milk. Stir in powdered sugar and vanilla. If necessary, thin with a few drops **milk.** Frosts 13x9 or 15x10-inch pan.

BROWNED BUTTER FROSTING

2 tablespoons butter
2 tablespoons milk or cream
2 cups powdered sugar
½ teaspoon vanilla

Brown butter in saucepan. Stir in milk, then the powdered sugar and vanilla. If necessary, thin with a few drops **milk** while frosting bars.

Frosts 13x9 or 15x10-inch pan.

PEANUT BUTTER FROSTING

2 tablespoons soft butter or margarine
2 tablespoons peanut butter
1 cup powdered sugar
1 to 2 tablespoons milk

Combine all ingredients, adding milk until of spreading consistency. Beat until smooth. Frosts 9x9, 10x8, 11x7, or 8x8-inch pan.

VANILLA FROSTING

2 tablespoons soft butter or margarine
2 tablespoons milk or cream
2 cups powdered sugar
½ teaspoon vanilla

Melt together butter and milk. Stir in powdered sugar and vanilla. Beat until smooth and creamy, adding more **milk,** if necessary. Frosts 13x9 or 15x10-inch pan.

SOUR CREAM FROSTING

¼ cup dairy sour cream
½ cup packed brown sugar
1¼ cups powdered sugar
¼ teaspoon vanilla

Heat together sour cream and brown sugar. Stir in powdered sugar and vanilla. Frosts 13x9 or 15x10-inch pan.

PENUCHE BROILED TOPPING

¾ cup packed brown sugar
½ cup chopped nuts or coconut
¼ cup soft butter or margarine
2 tablespoons milk

Combine all ingredients. Spread on bars; broil 2 to 5 minutes.

NUTMEG FROSTING

2 tablespoons butter or margarine
2 tablespoons cream or milk
1½ cups powdered sugar
¼ teaspoon rum flavoring
⅛ teaspoon nutmeg

Melt together butter and cream. Stir in remaining ingredients. Beat until smooth, adding more cream, if necessary. Frosts 13x9-inch pan.

COFFEE FROSTING

2 tablespoons butter or margarine
2 tablespoons milk
½ teaspoon instant coffee
1½ cups powdered sugar
½ teaspoon vanilla

Heat together butter, milk and coffee. Stir in powdered sugar and vanilla. Beat until smooth, adding more milk, if necessary. Frosts 13x9-inch pan.

WHIPPED CREAM TOPPINGS

MAKES: 1 cup

½ cup whipping cream
1 teaspoon sugar
½ teaspoon vanilla

Combine all ingredients in small mixing bowl. Beat until thick. Select variation below and fold into whipped cream. (For frozen topping, spoon individual serving into flat pan. Freeze. Serve frozen.)

Throughout this cookbook, you'll find suggested recipes to use as desserts. Whipped cream (just a little spoonful) adds a nice touch. Whipped cream is very special when you add a special flavor.

Strawberry Topping:
Fold ¼ cup **strawberry fruit filling** or **preserves** and 1 teaspoon **lemon juice** into whipped cream. (Raspberry and other preserves may be used.)

Orange Topping:
Fold ¼ cup **orange marmalade** and 1 teaspoon **lemon juice** into whipped cream.

Cinnamon Topping:
Beat into whipped cream ½ teaspoon **cinnamon**, ⅛ teaspoon **nutmeg** and 1 tablespoon **brown sugar.**

Applesauce Topping:
Increase **sugar** in whipped cream to 1 tablespoon. Fold in ¼ cup **applesauce** and ¼ teaspoon **cinnamon,** if desired.

Minted Whipped Cream:
Increase **sugar** to 1 tablespoon, then add ¼ teaspoon **mint flavoring** and 2 drops **red** or **green food coloring.**

Chocolate Whipped Cream:
Increase **sugar** in whipped cream to 2 tablespoons and add 1 tablespoon **cocoa** to cream before beating.

DESSERT COMBOS

Here are suggestions of dessert bars that are good with the Whipped Cream Toppings. Omit the frosting. Cut bars into about 3-inch squares and top with the whipped cream.

Strawberry Topping — Lemon Puffs, Lemon Nut Creams

Orange Topping — Lemon Cake Bars, Apple Quick Pie Bars, Sugar Squares

Cinnamon Topping — Spicy Pumpkin Bars, Golden Nuggets, Date Nut Creams, Banana Slims, Penuche Treasures

Applesauce Topping — Sugar 'N Spice Teacakes, Matrimonial Bars, Date Nut Squares, Gingersnap Chews

Minted Whipped Topping — Lemon Puffs

Chocolate Whipped Topping — Brownies (any recipe), Swiss Chocolate Dessert Bars, Luscious Tea Bars

A LITTLE TWIST

Many times it is just a little innovation or twist by the cook that wins praises. Instead of sprinkling unbaked cookies with plain sugar, try one of the **Flavored Sugars** below.

FLAVORED SUGARS

Combine 2 tablespoons **sugar** with one of the following:

½ **teaspoon cinnamon**	½ **teaspoon grated**
⅛ **teaspoon nutmeg or mace**	**orange peel**
	¼ **teaspoon grated lemon peel**

Cookies to use these sugars on are: Shortbread, Molasses Crisps, Old-Fashioned Sugar Cookies, "Spritz" Stix, Sugar Squares, Gingersnap Chews.

MAILING COOKIES

Any time is cookie time for the college student. Here are a few suggestions for making, baking and mailing cookies.

1. Select bar cookie recipes that are suitable for the destination. Do not bake fragile cookies for mailing. Also choose bars that stay fresh for several days.

2. Bar cookies are not only easy to bake, but easy to pack for mailing. Cut the bars into 4 or 5-inch squares and you won't have as many small cookies to wrap.

3. Select a good sturdy container for mailing. A metal one is excellent for overseas mailing.

4. Wrap each kind of cookie separately in plastic or foil. This way flavors and the moistness of cookies will not mingle.

5. Pack cookies tightly. Fill in extra spaces with crushed paper napkins. Popcorn is not recommended for packing when mailing cookies.

6. Wrap package securely. Print address clearly (remember to use zip code) on label and place on top side of package only.

7. Write or have post office stamp PERISHABLE on package. Special handling of package is possible for a small extra fee.

INDEX

NEW FAVORITES

COOKIE JAR FAVORITES

SWEET SHOPPE FAVORITES

FRUIT & PASTRY BARS

QUICK-AS-A-MIX FAVORITES

ALL TIME FAVORITES

COOKIE FROSTINGS